COMMERCIAL SPACE

Restaurants

COMMERCIAL SPACE

Restaurants

arco
editorial

AUTHOR
Francisco Asensio Cerver

EDITOR IN CHIEF
Paco Asensio

PROJECT COORDINATOR
Iván Bercedo (Architect)

PROOFREADING & TRANSLATION
INLINGUA. Techical Translations

GRAPHIC DESIGN & LAYOUT
Mireia Casanovas Soley

PHOTOGRAPHERS
Eduard Hueber (*Martinspark Hotel*); Lluís Casals (*Muffins*);
N. Ishii/Shinkentiku (*Asu-Kuju National Park*); Richard
Davis, C.Kicherer, Friedrich Busam (*Belgo Centraal*); Dito
Jacob (*Thèatron*); David Cardelús, Joan Mundó (*Little Italy*);
Mihail Moldoveanu (*Schirn*); Mihail Moldoveanu (*Gaig*);
Dennis Gilbert (*The Peoples Palace*); Alberto Ferrero (*La
Gare*); Mihail Moldoveanu, Herbé Ternissien (*Gavoille*);
Mihail Moldoveanu (*Iridium*)

Published and distributed by ROTOVISION SA
Sheridan House
112-116 A Western Road
Hove, East Sussex BN3 1DD
England
Tel. 1273 72 72 68
Fax 1273 72 72 69

Production and color separation in Singapore by
ProVision Pte. Ltd.
Tel: (065) 334-7720
Fax: (065) 334-7721

Restaurants are perhaps the commercial spaces which have the narrowest bond with our personal experience. They are intimately related to the memory of a date, a celebration, a journey, a city in which we have lived or a period in time.

The choice of restaurant provides a foretaste of what the evening holds. More important than the food is the type of atmosphere that is wished to be experienced. The restaurant acquires a ritualistic character and becomes a space of feelings. In our heads we keep a geography of restaurants that we intuitively relate with different moods and expectations. However, not all restaurants seek the same empathy with the customer. There are others that, in a more pragmatic line, only wish to fulfil their primary role, perhaps forming part of buildings with another function, such as museums, a concert hall or a station.

In the present volume we have tried to show concepts of completely different restaurants, intimate spaces and crowded premises, establishments located within the confines of a sky-scraper, in a national park, in a museum, in an old beer cellar, in a port, or next to a highway.

In the same way each one of the architects that appears in this volume takes on the setting up of a restaurant from a different angle. In the *Iridium* Jordan Mozer unfolds his fantasy, while in Felix and *Thèatron* we perceive the ability of Philippe Starck to equip spaces with a theatrical dimension. Masaharu Takasaki brings together architecture and cosmology in the restaurant in the national park *Asu-Kuju*. Ron Arad expresses his liking for industrial language in the remodelation of some ancient beer cellars. Kristian Gavoille pays homage to the world of cinema and theatre in the restaurant-cafeteria in the *Maison de la Culture in Amiens*. Josep Lluís García configures the space of the restaurant *Muffins* based on the intimate surroundings of the table. The architects of the Mohamed Salahuddin Consulting Engineering Bureau introduce a make-up of signs and neon lights as an expression of fast-food culture in the design of *Taco Maker*. Dietmar Eberle and Karl Baumschleger turn the restaurant of the *Martinspark Hotel* into a moored boat. Daniel Freixes and Vicente Miranda participate in the gradual renovation of the restaurant that they used to visit. Alfredo Arribas and Allies & Morrison design restaurants for a museum and an auditorium. Ismaele Morrone creates a vertiginous space in *La Gare* totally rejecting the existing space. Pilar Libano designs the interior of *Little Italy* with an ironic interpretion of fashion. Each architect contributes an irreducible personal look.

All the restaurants described here have been opened or reformed in recent years. We thus believe that the selection offers a global review of present design in spaces of this type.

Some of the spaces are located in Europe, others in America, the Middle East, Japan and Hong Kong.

Among the fourteen restaurants described here not one of them is the same. In this volume we wish to show examples of how to approach an architectural project from different angles and in which the results are equally valid.

Restaurants

▲ The Iridium is located opposite the
Lincoln Center in New York, in the
premises previously occupied by the
O'Neal Balloon. The design of the
Iridium was awarded the Spectrum
prize in 1994 for works which had
used ceramic materials, in the category

▶ View of the interior. All the
elements are endowed with a special
plasticity. Jordan Mozer was inspired by one
of the scenes from the Nutcracker ballet: "All

▲ According the architect, the copper roofs on 63rd Street take the form of the sound of a violin. The Iridium occupies two floors, in addition to the restaurant, there is also a Jazz club.

▼ Water colour perspective of the building where Iridium is located.

▼ Water colour drawing of the entrance to the premises.

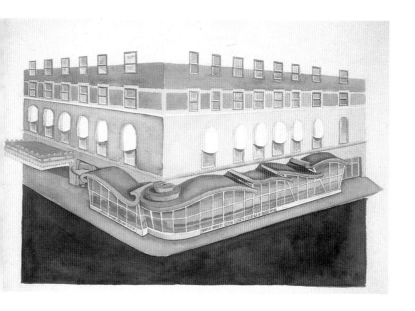

When crossing the threshold at Iridium it is no surprise to find a space which responds to the logic of a dream, of a poem or a musical piece. "Synaesthesia" is the word that rightly describes the sensation in which a sound evokes an image.

"What would music look like if it could be seen? Would the crescendos leave marks on the floor? What shape would the thumping of a drum take? Can the toilets execute a demi plié, or the copper tops a grand jeté? Imagine a table lamp in the middle of a pirouette. What image would a two-time harmony on the aluminium or a counterpoint on the clay have? If the arches were to give a bow on leaving the salon, would you applaud the architectonic final act? Goethe believed that architecture was akin to frozen music, what would music be like if it began to solidify?": Jordan Mozer presents the restaurant as a space in which

▲ *Shot of the entrance door. The Iridium evokes images reminiscent of Dalí through to Walt Disney, from Barishnykov and Antoni Gaudí to the Warner Brothers cartoons.*

▼ *General view of the interior. The furnishings were also designed by Jordan Mozer himself. The fabric on the sofas is patterned with images from the collages of Matisse. (A1)*

music and architecture melt together.

The Iridium is located between Columbus Avenue and Broadway, just on the other side of the Lincoln Center in New York. Jordan Mozer was inspired by the Nutcracker ballet: "Clara dreams of a romance, adventures and food. The salon becomes a surreal battlefield where she is attacked by a rat which, in the dream, becomes an enormous, hairy, many-headed warrior. Finally, her toy, a nutcracker,

▲ View of the bar and shot of the floor. The flooring mosaic, comprised of irregular stretches of broken tiles is inspired in the characteristic Antoni Gaudí trencadís style. (A2)

rescues her, transformed by the poetry of the REM into a handsome soldier who escorts her to a kingdom of crystalline fairies."

Jordan Mozer has created a place where the furnishings, the columns, doors and ceiling, indeed all the elements employed, must partake of the dance. The architect himself comments that just as in classical architecture, the Ionic columns are built inspired by a woman's figure, and the Doric columns on

▲ Ceiling shot. The lights are formed of different-shaped coloured glass pieces, like precious or magical stones.

15

◄ Design of the furniture is inspired by movements of ballerinas.

► Shots of the stools and chairs. The objects designed by Jordan Mozer constantly make reference to irony, thereby enhancing a relaxed, cheerful ambience.

▲ General view of the restaurant salon. The seat back represents a Pas de Deux.

► Water colour of one of the table lamps.

◄ *Shot of the stainless steel legs of one of the chairs and a dividing handrail. They are inspired by the legwarmers used by dancers and the points of ballet shoes.*

► *Each one of the cupboards takes a different position of a dancer. (A3)*

▼ *View of the Plácido Domingo column, which takes its name from the famous opera singer in the bullfighter role from Bizet's Carmen.*

masculine dimensions; the sculptural columns in the Iridium are formed based on the performers from the opera Carmen by Bizet (The column, Plácido Domingo in the role of bullfighter), and the furnishings trap the figures traced in the air by the dancers.

Though the forms in Iridium may appear to be somewhat haphazard, almost all of them transform images from the world of music and dance into architecture. Details from a violin, a clarinet, the leap of a dancer or even the lines of a musical score.

Jordan Mozer drew up a preliminary study of his works principally in sketches and models. When the latter were finished, Mozer worked in the company of a group of craftsmen specialising in making prototypes for each element on a larger scale, where all the technical aspects are already integrated, the finishes and materials. Each architectonic detail, each piece of furniture, each light, have been

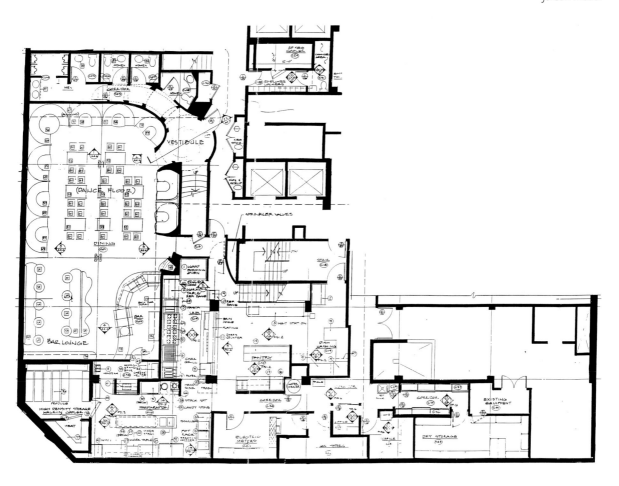

▲ *Plan of the ground floor.*

▼ *Plan of the first floor.*

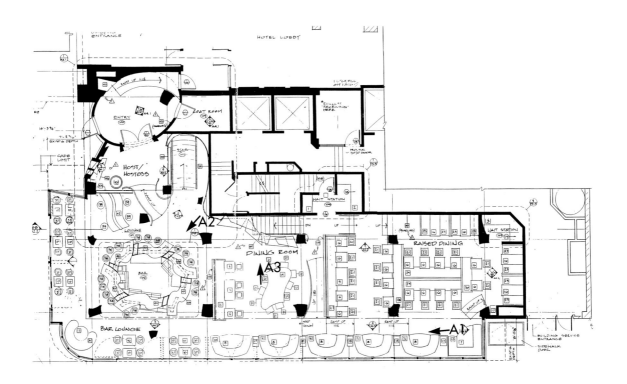

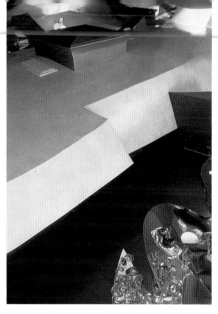

◀ *The colours range from reds, yellows, lilacs and purples, which unfurl in a gradual chromatic interplay. The red and yellow ceiling with twisted beams seems to be set on fire by the music.*

▼ *"I've been working on the idea of capturing music in architecture for at least ten years now" explained the architect from Chicago.*

individually designed. The follow through of the work was extraordinarily direct and specific. If this had not been so, it would have been almost impossible to carry out such a personal, singular work.

Mozer puts himself on the other side of Alice's looking glass. Goethe suggests that architecture is music frozen. ■

▲ *The hours of greatest activity
in the Iridium take place at night in the
main. It is strongly linked to the Lincoln
Center. It is mainly frequented by the
public wanting to have a drink
after a concert.*

MUFFINS

Josep Lluís García

▲ Entrance to the restaurant Muffins. Even on the façade, the architect has given great importance to the different forms of lighting. The transparencies and shadows looming through the translucent glass or the bright lighting of the niche holding the menu and the name of the restaurant. (A1)

▶ General view from the restaurant entrance. Advantage has been taken of the three pre-existing pillars to organise the ground floor. From the wall to each one of the pillars a wooden dividing screen has been placed which separates the ambience of each table. (B1)

Reformation of the Barcelona restaurant, Muffins, carried out by the architect Josep Luis Garcia, has managed to create a welcoming, intimate ambience, thanks to the choice of warm materials such as wood or the painstaking finishes, like the spatulate Venetian of the walls and the rigorous study of the lighting.

The restaurant is located in narrow, elongated premises which, with the stairway sited in the middle of the ground floor -

dividing the premises up into two floors of average height, means that the space is organised into three different levels. The entrance and bar having separate, independent characters.

The existence of an off-centre pillar has conditioned the design of the entrance design. Access is granted via a small, wood panelled exterior vestibule at the back of which there is a rectangular niche holding the menu, thus entrance to the establishment is perforce

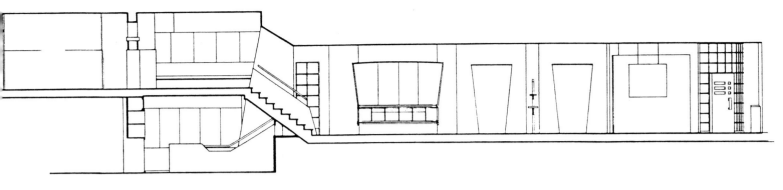

◀ *The stairway plays a vital role in the organisation of the floor. The premises are of a markedly longitudinal shape: narrow and deep. In the middle of the restaurant, two flights of stairs lead up to a salon situated on the lower floor and to another floor raised at half-floor height above the ground floor level. (B2)*

▲ *Longitudinal section through the premises where the distribution of the restaurant's three levels can be seen.*

▲ *General view of the lower floor. The kitchen is not totally enclosed. A wine rack separates it from the area set aside for the tables. (D1)*

25

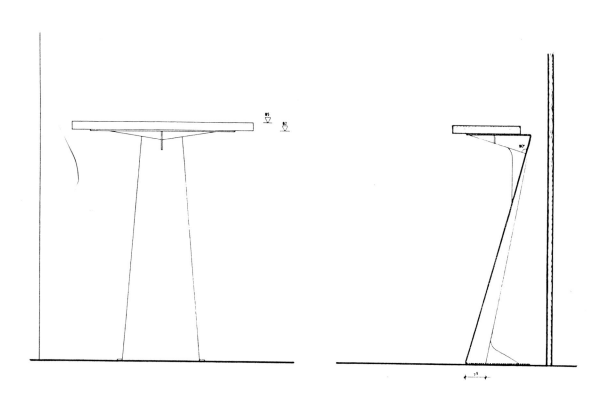

◀ *The tables are organised following a precise rhythm, marked out by some trapezoidally-shaped soffits fitted onto the wall. Each soffit is found directly related to one of the tables. (C1)*

▼ *Some of the furnishing elements, designed by the architect himself, bear a certain sculptural character. A shelf for putting the oil, salt or sugar bowl on becomes a piece of suggestive forms. (B3)*

▼ *Constructional detail of the covering used on the pillars.*

◀ *The architect has endeavoured to convey a cosy, intimate ambience. The materials, colours and finishes create a warm, tranquil atmosphere. The corners are taken advantage of to incorporate details, in this case, a small table-lectern with a rose on it.*

◀ *Detailed shot of the table-lectern.*

▼ *View of the entrance from the stairway. The shape of the restaurant has had to be moulded to the irregularities of the premises. Here, a counter can be seen in the foreground which adapts itself to a volume of the central box of the stairway which emerges out of the ground floor. The mirror visually duplicates the space. (B4)*

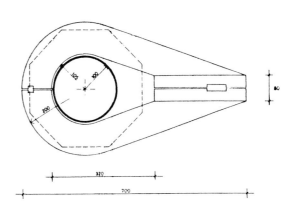

27

gained laterally, through a door cut out of an oblique translucent glass partition inspired by the architecture of C. R. Mackintosh.

Between the entrance and the restaurant itself it was thought suitable to create a transitional space, the bar, where customers could wait in the event of all the tables being occupied.

The dividing up of the restaurant into three floors at different heights makes it possible for the spaces to be more cosy, given that the salons are relatively small, with a seating capacity for between twenty and thirty diners.

On the ground floor, the central passageway divides two rows of tables on each side. In one of the rows, a succession of three

▼ *Lighting has been one of the most painstakingly studied factors when designing the restaurant. The light from the lamps situated behind the soffits, perimetrally, provokes the sensation of them being floating free of the wall, in mid-air as it were.*

pre-existing pillars allows the space to be organised around the four independent tables, separated by the pillars themselves and by three wooden screens at the eye level of a seated diner.

Instead of trying to disguise the presence of the three pillars, they have instead been given a role in configuring the salon. They have been covered with sand-washed steel sheeting, giving them a greater volume and singular form.

The ceiling is in the somewhat lower strip, which helps it to state itself as an independent area.

On both the gallery floor and the lower floor great effort has been made to make the layout of the tables as flexible as possible, thereby enabling the capacity to cater for large dinner parties, business dinners or banquets. That is why the false ceiling is perforated metal sheeting in both salons. Above the sheeting, a large amount of waiting points for the lighting in accord with the versatility of these floors.

The restaurant kitchen is located on the lower floor and is separated from the table area by means of a bottle rack which in turn also allows the irregularities of the wall to be absorbed.

Every effort has been made to ensure that the tables are sheltered, resting up against a wall, a handrail or a tall piece of furniture, thus making sure that one of its sides is partitioned off. In a place with such limited space it is absolutely vital to "own" at least a small amount of the space to feel protected, calm and comfortable. This then is the reason for which the architect has considered it so important to configure, within the general space, several independent settings of a small area, and has even managed to create a particular ambience around each table.

On the walls next to the rows of tables, a rhythmic succession of trapezoidally-shaped wooden soffits has been created. These soffits are set slightly apart from the wall with the aim of housing perimetral lighting which gives a certain volumetric character. This creates a successive overlapping of planes which alternate light and shadow: the light pink coloured wall, lit from inside the soffit, the DM veneered and ruddily hued varnished soffit, as

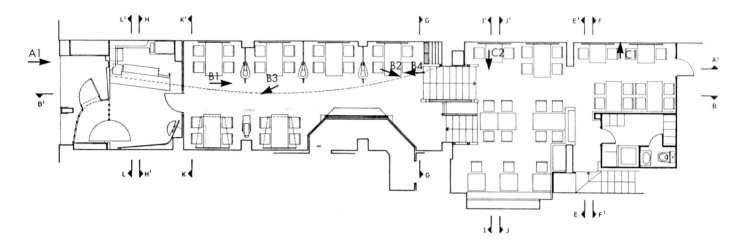

▲ Plan of the ground floor and gallery.

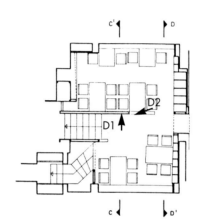

◀ Plan of the lower floor. The kitchen has not been reformed in the project carried out by Josep Luis Garcia.

▼ View of the ground floor from the gallery. The flooring is done using graphite grey 30 x 30 cm tiles. The walls are finished in a salmon coloured Venetian spatulate. The handrails, soffits and screens are reddish stained DM.

backlighting, and, lastly, the ray of light thrown out by an applique situated in the centre of the soffit.

Above each one of the tables there is a chromed lamp with a conical head. The height and form of the lamp has been especially studied so that it lights the table without blinding the diners. At the end of the brace there is a jack which can be plugged into the different waiting points in the ceiling to enable flexibility when laying out the tables and to avoid the lighting being off centre.

On the lower floor it was not possible to fit the restaurant's characteristic soffits owing to the retaining wall's profile. In this case, a linear wooden element has been opted for. ■

▲ *View of the lower floor. As the restaurant has been divided into three floors, the rooms turn ont to the cosier. They are relatively small spaces for no more than thirthy diners. In contrast to the ground floor, the lay-out of the tables on the gallery floor and lower floor allows greater versatility. (D2)*

FELIX RESTAURANT

Philippe Starck

▲ General view of the main salon of
the restaurant. The Long Table,
especially illuminated, in the
background. On special occasions this
can be used to organise shows or

► Shot of one of the tables of the
restaurant . The furnishings, designed by
Philippe Starck himself, constitute one of the
attractions of the Felix. The tables are marble.
The white-upholstered chairs are the Vitra

In Hong Kong, one of the cities with the greatest variety of superlative images on Earth, the fantastic becomes merely a matter of course. The centre suffers from an ever growing density of excessive buildings, subjected to the surprising acceleration of a series of wagers bordering on the unimaginable. In this place, built with boundless architecture, after Norman Foster's Bank of Hong Kong and Pei's Bank of China, the latest provocation, the space admired by seekers of breathtaking images, is found on the twenty-eighth floor of the Peninsula Hotel, a restaurant: Felix.

The Peninsula, one of the city's most well-known hotels, was converted after the Second World War, under the guidance of Leo Gaddi, into a reference point in the city. Its prestige has not been perturbed in the least with the passing of time. To crown the recent extension, the aim was to install on the highest floor a different restaurant, with a leisurely character and innovative, attractive image which would quickly become an identifiable, emblematic space. In the words of its promoters: "A twenty-first century brasserie." The name, Felix, comes from one of its historical directors, Felix M. Bieger.

When customers reach the Peninsula's lobby and wait for the lift to go up to the Felix on the twenty-eighth floor, they know that on getting there they are not going to enjoy the dinner alone, but are instead going to be witnesses to a show. Nevertheless, what is going to surprise them is not, as to be expected, the view out over the city or the outline of the Kowloon mountain, but is another show instead, images of another kind.

The city is seen as a backdrop, in the background, unfocused and blurred through the screens covering the enormous windows, veiled by the impact of what is taking place in the restaurant itself which, thus, superimposing

▲ *General view of the restaurant's main salon from The Long Table, together with the kitchen. In the background the two symmetrical towers housing the discotheque and the bars.*

itself on the presence of the surrounding city, becomes the centre, in the only place where things happen.

This scenario is somewhat reminiscent of the first night at an opera in the last century, or of a New York ballroom in the twenties: it moves the protagonism of the activity in course to the show in which you take part.

Felix is not merely a restaurant, but is instead a series of spaces where dining, drinking an apéritif, tasting a mature vintage wine, dancing or simply having a drink are possible. Each space constitutes an independent setting, each one having a name identifying it: The Main Restaurant, The Long Table, The American Bar, The Balcony, The Private Room, The Wine Bar and the Crazy Box.

The restaurant is roughly rectangular in shape, this being determined by the floor plan of the hotel. The perimeter, however, is configured with large, curved windows which trace a sinuous outline. At both ends of the floor there are two wells for lifts and stairways,

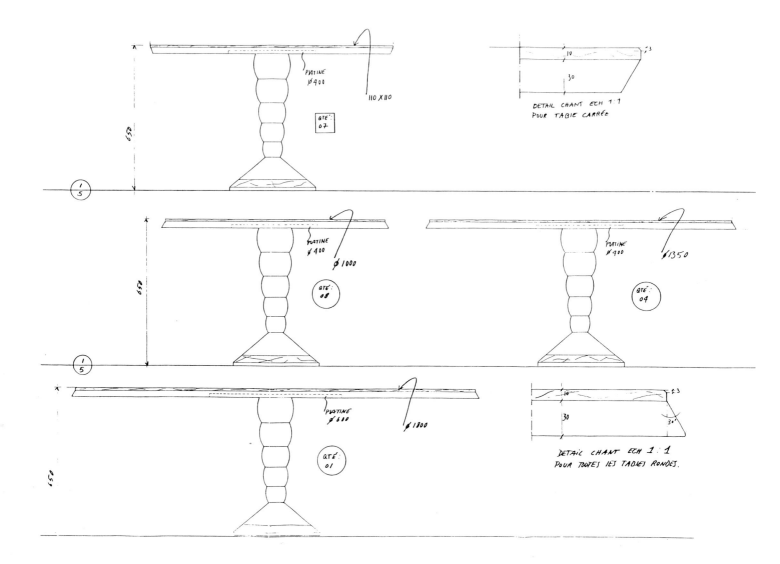

PATINE ⌀ 400

110 X 110

QTÉ 07

DETAIL CHANT ECH 1:1
POUR TABLE CARRÉE

PATINE ⌀ 400

⌀ 1000

QTÉ 08

PATINE ⌀ 400

⌀ 1350

QTÉ 04

PATINE ⌀ 600

⌀ 1800

QTÉ 01

DETAIL CHANT ECH 1:1
POUR TOUTES LES TABLES RONDES.

▲ *Shot of the restaurant tables.*

each one of which is assigned a different function: one constitutes the natural entrance to the restaurant, while the other is linked to the kitchen. The line joining both ends becomes the main axis of the restaurant and determines a symmetrical layout of both sides. Prior to reaching the main room of the restaurant, customers go through two spiral-shaped towers covering two floors which house The Wine Bar and The American Bar, two settings where apéritifs and vintage wines are served prior to dining, and another two spaces, The Balcony and The Crazy Box, there for those who, having dined, wish to have a drink or dance.

The main salon, with seating capacity for 101 diners, is conceived as a large space with a

▲ Shot of the two stairways that lead up to the second floor of the towers. One stairway seen from the other. The artificial lighting is one of the most important elements for qualifying the spaces. Felix is preferentially a nightspot.
In many places, Starck has illuminated the floor, such as the stairways, for example.

double-height giving one sole ambience, with round tables distributed throughout the entire floor space with no exact order to them. At the back, visible anywhere in the restaurant, Philippe Starck has sited an enormously long table - The Long Table - which can be used by both the customers and as a setting to organise shows or fashion parades. ■

▲ General view of The Wine Bar. Wine can be tasted here while waiting to dine. It is a small space, with the appearance of a wine cellar capable of holding 12 people. The walls are covered with bottles.

► *Shot of The Wall Wine Bar with the bench set up against the wall. In this setting, the zinc of the walls has been combined with the wooden benches and tables.*

▼ *Constructional detail of The Wall Wine Bar.*

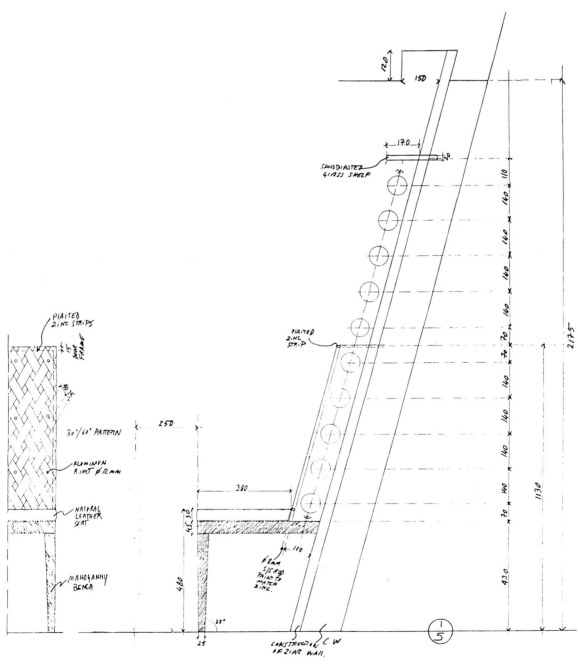

▲ General view of The American Bar, on the second floor of one of the towers. The central bar facilitates interaction between the customers. It can hold up to 34 people.

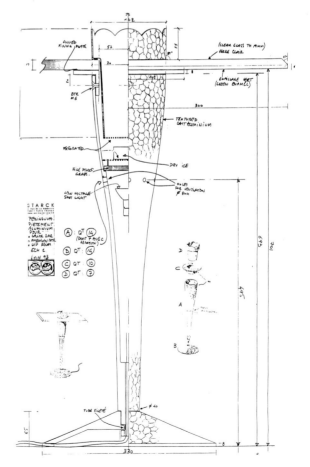

▶ Detail of the aluminium table legs of The American Bar and the Balcony.

◄ The Balcony is somewhat similar in appearance to The American Bar. It is located on the second floor of the other tower. The tables and chairs are aluminium. It is designed for those wishing to have a drink after dining and can hold up to 21 people.

▼ Detailed plans of The Crazy Box.

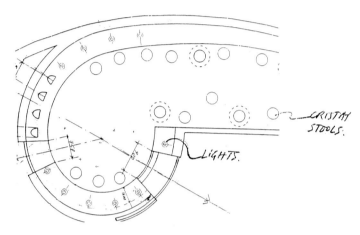

POSITION OF LIGHTS IN DISCO. SCALE $\frac{1}{50}$

PATTERN OF UPHOLSTERY AND POSITION OF LIGHTS IN DISCO

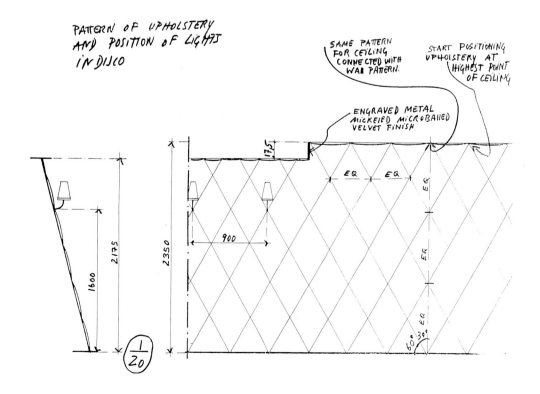

▶ *A view of the discothèque, called The Crazy Box, with a capacity for up to 20 people. It is sited on the lower floor of one of the towers, hence, its characteristic spiral shape.*

▲ *View of the gentlemen's rest room. A large marble table located in the centre of the room is used as the communal washbasin. The curiously shaped taps are reminiscent of rèptiles.*

41

▲ Despite having more than 300m²
floor space, it is organised using three
decorative elements solely: a large
frame approximately ten metres high
and six wide, containing a photograph
of Richard Avedon, a large stairway
and a grey velvet curtain with the
reverse side being done in scarlet silk -
more than 12 m high and 16 m wide.

▶ General view of the vestibule.
The Thèatron is essentially divided up into
three spaces: the Vestibule, the Restaurant
and the Bar. The restaurant can seat up to
280 diners, while the bar can hold up to

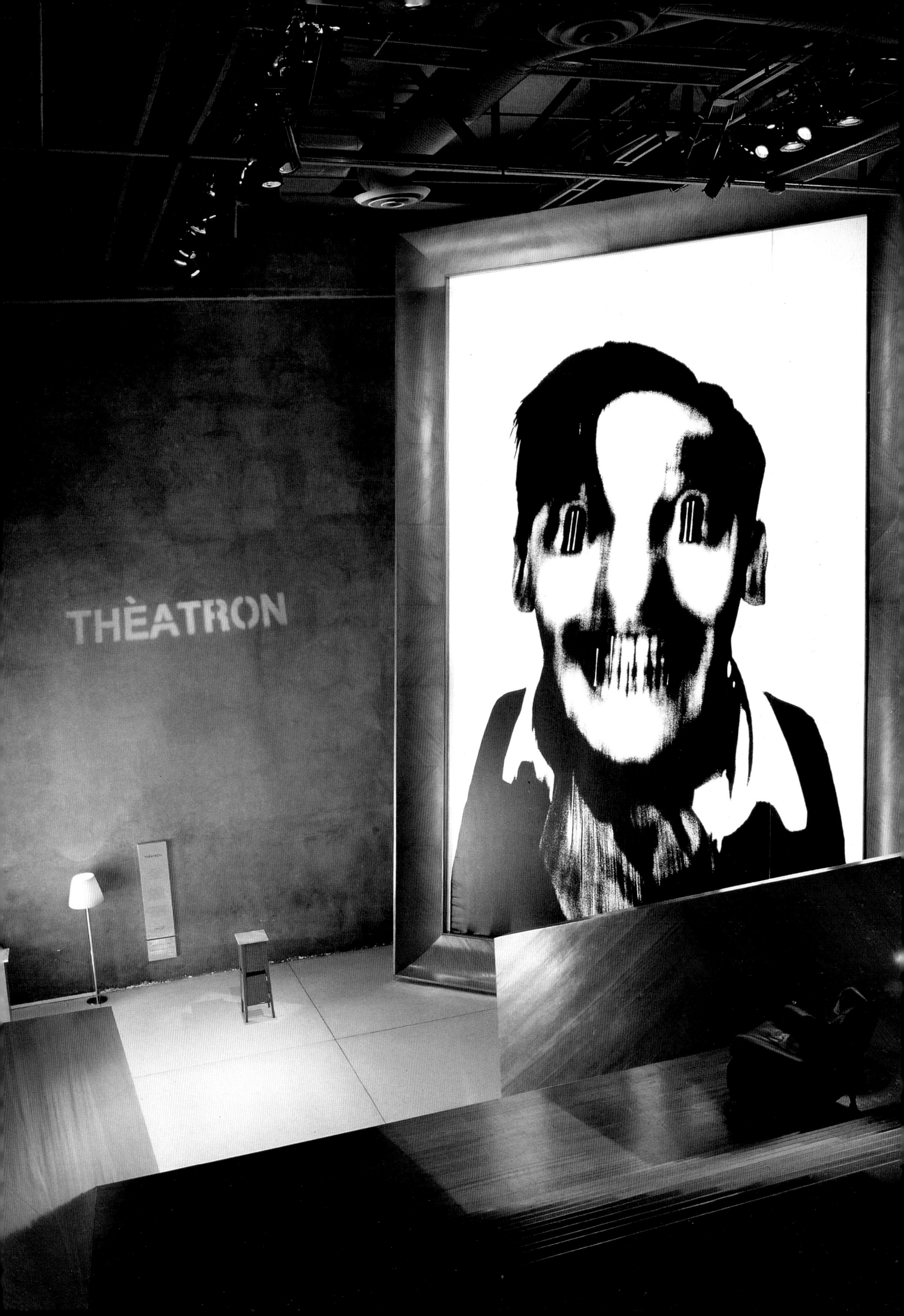
THÈATRON

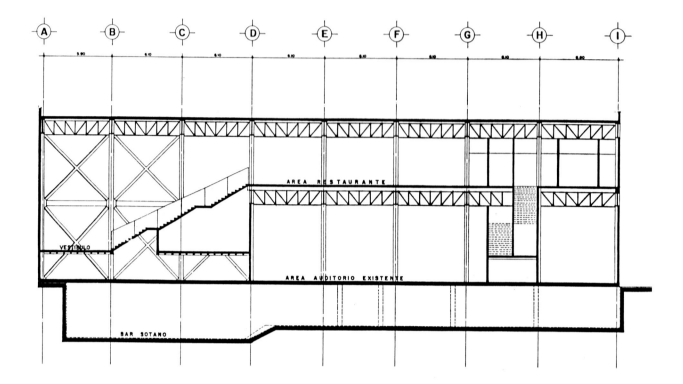

Like the Teatriz in Madrid or the Felix in Hong Kong, the Thèatron restaurant in the city of Mexico, has a scenographic character which goes beyond its immediate function. The customers do not go to the restaurant only to dine, have a drink or wile the evening away, they go to the Thèatron so that the night attains its maximum theatricality. The customers become the protagonists in their own acts. And they do so in an entirely different manner to how it is done in other restaurants or at other dinners.

This "reflecting upon oneself" that Rimbaud talked about and, subsequently, the existentialists from Heidegger to Camus, that self conscience which is superimposed over ones own self, that is the territory where Starck throws those who pass through his architectural pieces. He does this, however, in the opposite direction to the existential angst, doing coming from irony and play. The spaces designed by Philippe Starck do not have their

roots in reality, they do not operate on the landscape or on the volumetric compositions, but on the collective imagination instead. They are endogamic spaces, but with an introversion more radical yet than simple hermetism towards the exterior or surroundings, they dialogue only with the 0visual heritage of the visitors.

His architecture links together a series of different places which reach their sense through the passages they foster. However, as opposed to the promenade architecturel of Le Corbusier, these passages do not have spatial identity, they do not relate how they are passed through, neither do they make any reference to the relative positions of some points with respect to others, nor do they articulate in order to express the ultimate poetry of their own movements; Starck's are promenades imaginaires, they take place between memorised images, cinematographic sequences, mixed up one with the other and

◀ *Section.*

▲ *View of the stairway leading up to the restaurant, built using tropical wood. In a central rest area, Starck has put a solitary armchair, next to table with a lamp on it.*

▲ General view of the restaurant or
the Cielo (Heaven) as it is called by
Starck. Its floor space covers
approximately 1,200 m², including the
services and kitchen. Some translucent
curtains made in Tergal which stop
1.20 m short of the floor divide the
space up into different settings. (B2)

► Level -5.90 plan.

► Level -2.20 plan.

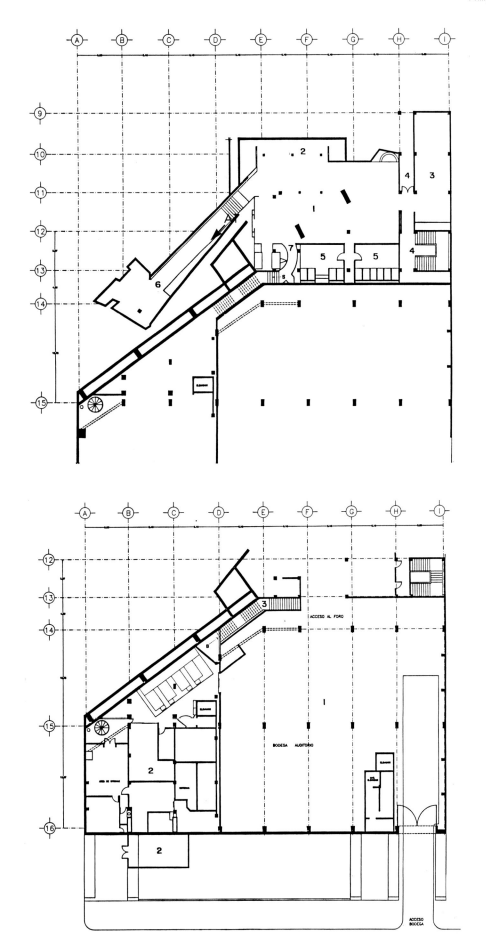

▼ The Thèatron is located in the National Auditorium and is brainchild of Philippe Starck. The project has been carries out by the French designer, while management of the work has been done by the Mexican architect, baltasar Vez. (B4)

distilled out into astonishing scenarios.

Starck brings back the best of impressionism. In his buildings, references are found not only to Einsentein, Murnau, Fritz Lang or Welles, but we also find that same capacity to extend reality out over the territory of dreams, of anguishes and feelings. However, as opposed to what happened in the works of the others, in Starck's what rips apart reality is not tragedy but irony instead.

The spaces overflow with humour, the scenographics have a leisurely character, are

▶ In the main, the furnishings are designed by Starck, combining with period furniture and chandeliers of more than 2.50 m in height. (B3)

48

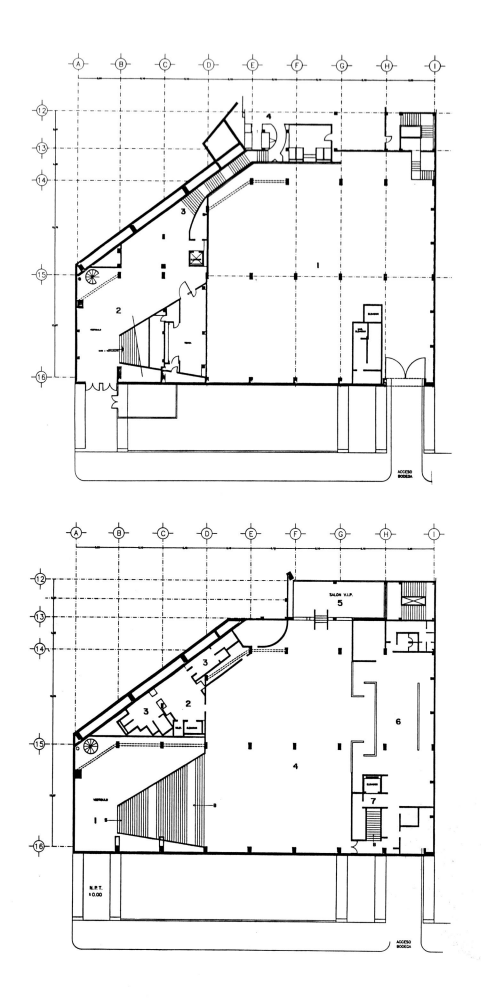

inoffensive. They look for the complicity of the spectator. All those going to dine at the Thèatron or the Felix attend to take part in this game. One salon is lit by a nineteenth century chandelier, the next by bulb suspended by a cable from the ceiling. Diners go up a monumental, disproportionate stairway, and then go along a dimly lit narrow passageway. The restaurant salon is submerged in a hazy atmosphere: some white diaphanous curtains snake around the spaces from the ceiling down to chair height, thus only half-dividing the space. From each one of the settings one is conscious of there being other similar ones which extend further beyond, but it is impossible to have a complete idea of them, their presence, their spectre can only be guessed at.

Like the Pop artists, Starck returns to well-known images ranging from the paradoxical to the ironical, in his case, however, they are not

▲ *Shot of the rest room. A large mirror presides over this space, which, both for its finishes and furnishings is completely unlike conventional rest rooms.*

◄ *Level +0.30 plan.*

◄ *Level +5.65 plan.*

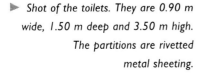

▶ *Shot of the toilets. They are 0.90 m wide, 1.50 m deep and 3.50 m high. The partitions are rivetted metal sheeting.*

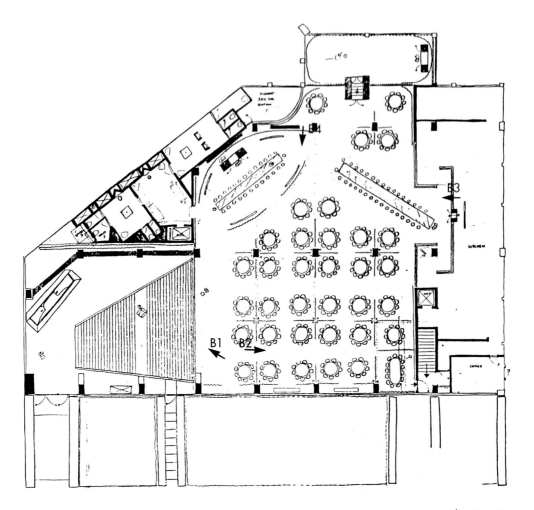

▲ Main floor.

▼ In the bar area objects can be found designed by Eames, Terragni, Dalí, Donghia and period pieces, in what becomes an authentic furniture museum.

outside of us, in society: comics, popular faces, everyday consumer items... Though he rescues his scenographics from the collective imagination, Starck's architectures imply the individual, converting them into actors and making them play with their own imagination. Hence, those going to dine are actors in their own acts, but they do so in a different way as it is all taking place in their own conscience, in the inverse direction to existentialism: the conscience is doubled over in reality. ■

▲ *View of one of the bar's salons, or the*
Infierno (Hell) as it is called by Starck.
It is situated on the ground floor and
covers approximately 500 m². The
flooring and walls are covered with
tropical woods.

▲ *View of the Billiard room. The lighting consists of a bulb suspended from a cable. Starck always looks to surprise, and is just as likely to use a chandelier as a single, naked bulb.*

◀ *Shot of the "Crazy-Box", a tunnel with fluorescent flooring and padded walls, especially designed as a dance area.*

SCHIRN

Alfredo Arribas Arquitectos Associados

◢ *Shot of the bar. The gentle hues of the wood and the whiteness of the plaster dominate the atmosphere throughout the entire cafeteria.*

▶ *The Schirn cafeteria restaurant is found in the historical centre of Frankfurt am Main, on the ground floor of the Schirn Kunsthalle. (A1)*

◄ *Shot of the bar. The bar almost reaches the main entrance, dividing the circulation into two different directions. (A2)*

► *General view of the interior of the bar. At a lower level to the bar, another stainless steel counter is used by the waiters. The refrigerators are located under this second counter.*

▼ *View of the false ceiling where the lighting for the bar has been installed. The false ceiling protrudes like a phalanx over the triple-height space of the entrance. (A3)*

► *General layout of the cafeteria restaurant.*

The cafetería restaurant designed by the Catalan architect, Alfredo Arribas, is located on the ground floor of the Schirn Kunsthalle, the Frankfurt am Main art gallery, found in the historical centre of the Hesse Lander capital. The cafetería is accessed from both the gallery and the street, thereby enabling it to run independently.

The design of the establishment's interior has its origins in the interpretation of the existing building. The new elements transform the space. Each piece moulding the emptiness, moves it, gathers it or sinuously wraps it, as if it were a topography. The interior unfurls a series of filled and empty spaces both conceived as counterpoised corporeal elements. Yet, nevertheless, the volumes flow and are outlined over the triple-height space. The air traces runs between the volumes, connecting the spaces, like water flowing through communicating vessels. Like the duality

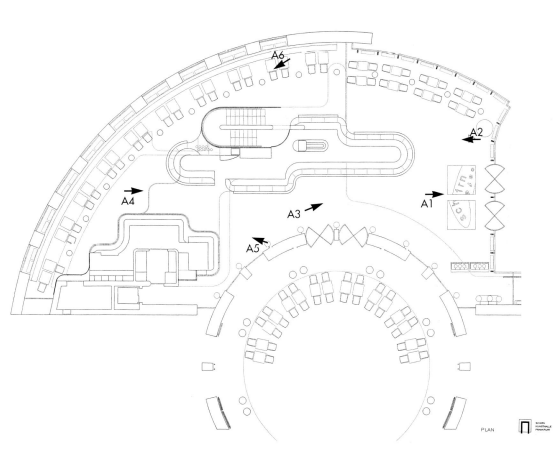

PLAN

SCHIRN
KUNSTHALLE
FRANKFURT

of Yin and Yang, the dialectic does not establish logical consequences, but instead solely unfolds an emotive passage.

The height of the spaces varies in a stepped fashion. The entrance is via an 11 m high glassed in gallery, a triple space. All along the rest of the circular façade, a narrow strip reaches up to a two-floor height, while the central space, around the bar and the kitchen, is rather low.

The warped wooden surfaces of different heights are reminiscent of the Finnish pavilion designed by Alvar Aalto for the 1939 New York exhibition. Arribas once again takes advantage of the possibilities offered by wood to create a warm atmosphere of organic contours.

Arribas has built the floor around a few clearly defined elements. The bar occupies the centre of the space. Built next to the volume of the stairway, faced with wooden panels, the counter unfurls like a snaking ribbon which advances almost right up to the entrance and

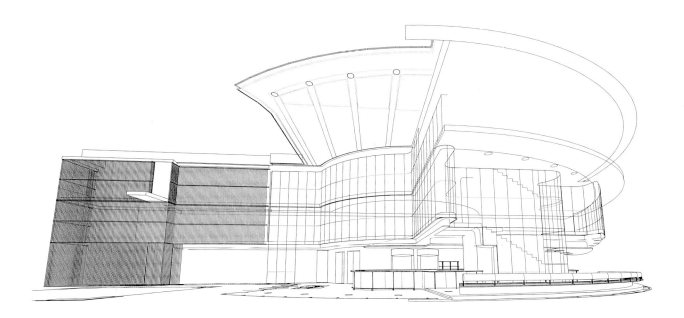

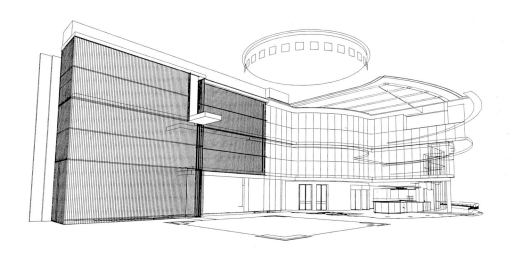

▲ *General perspective rendered by*
computer.

◀ *The bar occupies the centre of the*
space. Rather than a furnishing
element, it constitutes an authentic
architectonic piece with a fundamental
importance in the organisation of the
space.

▲ *General perspective.*

61

▶ *General view of the cafeteria.
The snaking ribbon of the bar shapes
itself to the volume of the stairway
which leads up to the upper floor. (A4)*

▼ *The flooring is dark oak wood
parquet. On the false ceiling, the
openings for the ventilation grilles and
lighting, attractive patterns unfold over
the plasterwork.*

then turns back on itself through 180°, to return to its original starting point, enclosing an area staffed by the waiters. This phalanx which almost reaches the main entrance divides the circulation and separates the floor into two different spaces.

All along the façade, a series of tables have been aligned, closely linked to the exterior by large vertical windows. The rhythm of the tables follows the layout of the windows. Next to the wall, Arribas has designed a bench covered with ivory-coloured leather. The tables are pear wood with glass tops which bear the cafeteria's logotype. This space is double-floor height and is a few metres wide, which provokes a particular impression. The end of this strip of the tables, the end nearest the kitchen, corresponds to the restaurant area.

On the other side of the bar, the cafeteria opens out toward an exterior rotunda where some tables have been put. The kitchen is found at one end of the premises, right on the other side of the entrance door. This is a space of rounded contours faced with stainless steel panels, an almost free element which, just like the bar, could be considered as an independent piece.

The materials used in the Schirn cafeteria restaurant convey a sensation of silence and tranquillity. The elements introduced by Arribas try to integrate themselves in the general ambience of the Kunsthalle. On this occasion, the visual effects have been left in the art gallery.

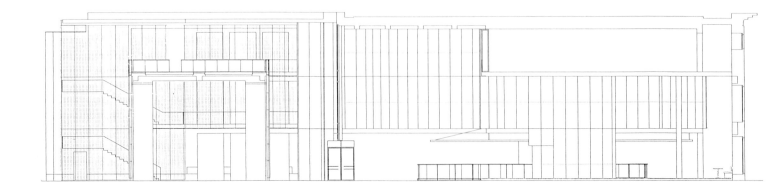

▲ *In the section, the different heights of the spaces can be appreciated.*

▶ *Shot of the bar with the kitchen volume in the background. As can be seen, though there is no direct relationship between the kitchen and bar, the latter is equipped with all the elements required to prepare apéritifs.*

◀ *Shot of the counter around the kitchen. The volume of the kitchen is faced with stainless steel. (A5)*

▶ *General view of the strip where the tables are sited. This area is directly linked with the exterior via the vertical windows. The bench is leather upholstered. The pear wood tables have glass tops. (A6)*

a Gare restaurant (The
is situated immediately
ath Milan's central railway

View of the restaurant. La Gare
includes a restaurant, discotheque and bar.
Though the discothèque and restaurant areas
are in fact separated, both share the same

The project designed by Ismaele Morrone for the restaurant-bar-discothèque La Gare de Milan is completely detached from the existing space on which it is designed. Its conception is entirely opposed, what is more, it implies its negation.

La Gare is situated in old premises covering 1000 m², located right underneath Milan's central railway station. The space is divided up into three clearly defined areas separated by thick loadbearing walls: enormous empty, square-floored salons, roofed with lowered barrel vaulted ceilings.

Morrone, instead of trying to fill, divide or furnish the salons, has thought the project through as one sole space, ignoring the walls. The rigidity of the existing space was very far indeed from the idea he had of how La Gare should be: a dynamic, leisurely, vertiginous place, of fluid spaces mixed up one with the other fostering movement.

However, the architect from Bergamo went one stage further: he threw down a radical

challenge, to negate the tectonic, the physical.

"... the interior space is completely black to annul its physical presence" states Ismaele Morrone. Both the vaulted ceilings and the floor and walls are pitch black, so much so that the outlines of the space become vague like the night.

Morrone proposes an architecture of different guidelines, improbable angles and brilliant, intense colours: red, blue, pink. In his own words "these elements are not a casual expressionist form, nor do they respond to a search for any mathematical topology; they are elemental forces disconnected from images and contents, purged of any contaminating influences, outside of space and time." Each element is generated by a striking force, with a whiplash.

The architect believes that "using this force, the project breathes life into a real space, physically formed by material extended with pure lines, elements, which by their very

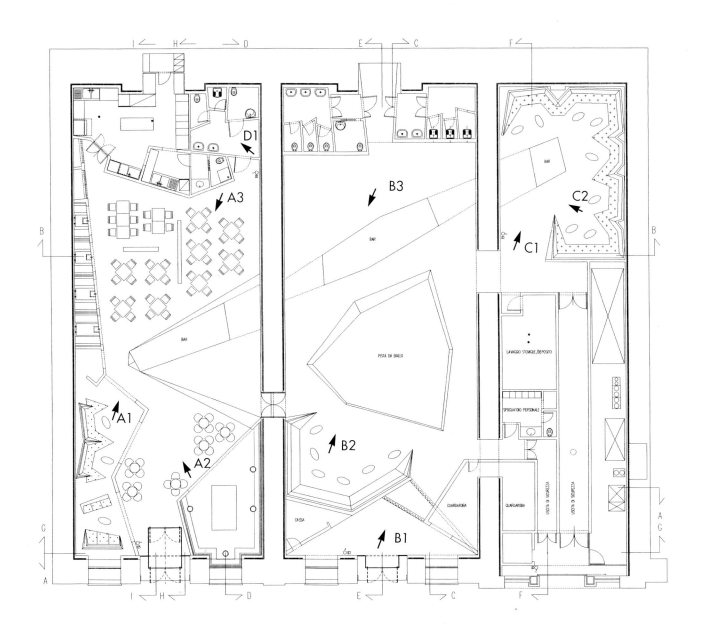

▲ General floor plan layout plan.

◀ The vaulted roofs have been faced over with metal panels. The floor covered with concrete poured in situ with an oxide and transparent water-repellant resin finish. Both the vaulted ceilings and the floor are pitch black which dematerialises the outlines, transforming the tectonic into darkness. (A2)

▲ General view of the restaurant, with the tables in the foreground and the bar and reserved spaces in the background. Ismaele Morrone has used intensely coloured elements: red, blue, white,... which stand out against the black background. (A3)

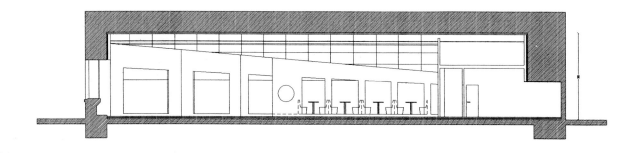

▲ Longitudinal section through the restaurant.

simplicity, become free of their own immovable mass and become articulated in a movement which convulses everything: space, things, people."

The result is a virtual architecture, which only makes sense from the state of animation of those who are going to use this establishment. La Gare conjoins three distinct activities, the restaurant, the bar and the discothèque. Nevertheless, both the leisure nature, which fosters the deinhibition of the customer, and the nocturnal hours kept, is common to all the ambiences offered.

The discothèque and restaurant are separate and have independent entrances. In fact, the restaurant corresponds to one of the existing bays of the premises. The desire of the promoters of La Gare, however, is that the customers go from one part to another, that the division between activities is translated into extending the customers' stay there. The idea

▲ *The Bar's red volume is constructed using a tubular structure covered inside by fireproof wood panels with plastic finish, the exterior being covered with gypsum-board and plaster panels, lacquered with gloss acrylic paint.*

▶ *Shot of one of the restaurant's reserved areas. Certain references to the railway aesthetic can be detected here: the same type of seats and dimensions similar to those of a railway carriage.*

is that those going to dine there do not leave the establishment for the rest of the night, but instead spend the night dancing or drinking while sitting on the sofas situated in some corner of the premises. The bar, constructed in an intense red colour, runs through the three spaces and thus becomes the uniting element between them.

Thus, this force and dynamism which pervades throughout, according to Ismaele Morrone, coincides with the state of animation which is trying to be fostered. Paradoxically, the less use made of Cartesian architecture with the use of a more excessive style, wich gathers the most hilarious forms the imagination, ends up by being the most functional. ■

▲ *General view of the discothèque.
In the foreground, some seats, in the
middle, the dance floor with the bar in
the background. The dance floor is set
at a lower level with the aim of
defining its outline. (B2)*

◀ *View of the discothèque entrance,
with the cloakroom space on the right.
Both the restaurant and discothèque
have independent entrances. There is,
however, an interior door connecting
both spaces. (B1)*

▼ *Transversal section, where the vaulted ceiling of the three spaces can be clearly appreciated. The maximum height of the vaults is 5.85 m and the width between walls, 11.25 m.*

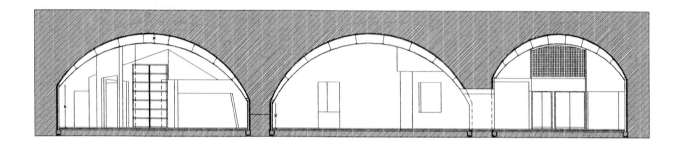

▼ *Shot of the discothèque bar. The bar is a red oblique piece which runs through the three bays, thereby establishing continuity between all the spaces. (B3)*

▼ *General view of the bar. In the narrowest bay, all of the installations have been fitted. However, full advantage has been taken of one of the ends to put a bar with a more intimate, tranquil ambience. (C1)*

◀ Shot of the bar. The sharp-angled forms try to convey dynamism to the space. They are forceful lines which run through the different areas. (C2)

▼ Shot of the rest rooms. The restaurant toilets are also converted into a rhetorical space. Painted in an intense yellow, broken up shapes and with spotlights set into the floor, they are designed in the same spirit as the rest of the establishment. (D1)

▲ The work that has been carried
out in the Gaig restaurant has not only
radically changed the atmosphere of
the establishment, but has also caused
modifications in the type of cuisine and
in the profile of the clientele.

▶ General view of one of the
rooms in the restaurant with the garden
in the background. The decision of the
owners to make use of the back court of
the restaurant meant a series of changes

◀ Detail of the facade of the restaurant. The house in which Gaig is located is an old two-storey building . The entrance is through the door on the right, the door on the left leads to the living quarters upstairs.

▲ View of the restaurant from the entrance. A set of shelves with books and bottles separates a small waiting room from the restaurant. The plant on the shelves provides a reference to the back garden with its ivy-covered walls. (A1)

▶ General floor plan of the restaurant.

The restaurant has a narrow, lengthened shape. The central walkway allows a complete view of the premises from the entrance to the back garden.

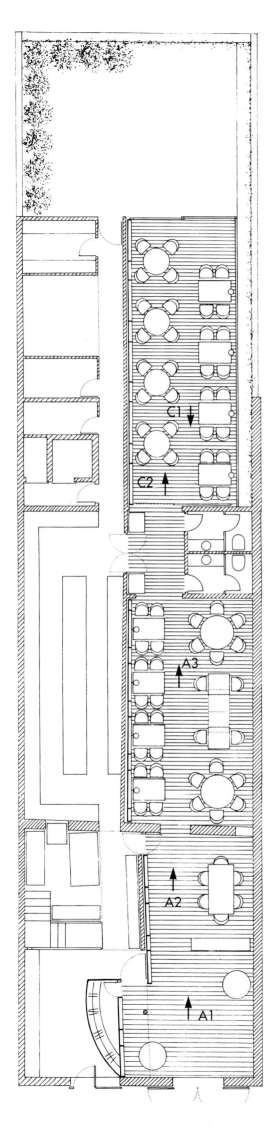

Daniel Freixes & Vicente Miranda

Reformation of the Barcelona Gaig restaurant is the story of a slow transformation, carried out over a twelve-year period, in successive interventions which have not only changed the restaurant's image, but also the type of cuisine, the hours kept and the profile of the clientele.

Though the decision to give a new character to a restaurant oftentimes carries with it a reforming of the premises, in the case of the Gaig is different, given that here the changes are as a result of a chain of initiatives, of a dialectic interchange between the architects, the owner and the clientele. Each modification took place as a consequence of the previous change, hence, starting from a small intervention, twelve years later, the restaurant now presents an entirely different image.

The Gaig restaurant was the place where the architects Dani Freixes and Vicente Miranda used to eat almost daily: a typical

◀ *The wall that separates the restaurant from the area of kitchens, storerooms and freezers is covered with okume wood panels. (A2)*

▼ *Detail of the tables. The yellow light on the reddish wood surfaces is reflected in gilt tones.*

▼ *The restaurant is divided into various rooms which are joined successively. The architects have introduced various elements that separate them, such as the washrooms, or they have made use of the existing walls of the house with the aim of obtaining spaces that are cosier and more well proportioned. (A3)*

establishment providing home cooking, highly frequented at midday by all those who worked in the area, but which was almost entirely empty at night.

An extremely simple first decision, to take advantage of the patio at the back of the restaurant, favoured people coming to eat during the hot summer nights. The nocturnal clientele demanded a different type of cuisine. More original dishes were introduced, these in turn attracting more selective clients. A change of furnishings and better finishes and lighting were required. Both the owner and architects decided on the reformations in according with each year's experiences and these were carried out during the holiday month when the restaurant was closed. Twelve years later, one restaurant has replaced the other, without any drastic rupture having taken place.

The Gaig is located on the ground floor of an old, two-floored house. A structural wall

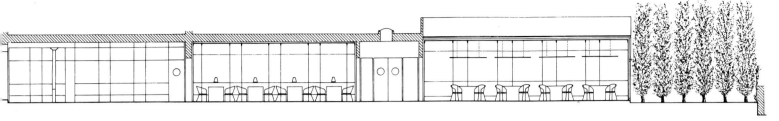

divides the premises in half, this extends almost right to the end of a narrow, elongated plot. The restaurant's successive salons are located in one of the two bays, with the other housing all the services: the kitchen, cold storage rooms, the stores and access to the upper floor. The bay housing the salons is 2.5 m wide and 18 m in depth approximately. This obliged the architects to provide several separative elements, with the aim of breaking up the continuity of the space and to create smaller, more proportional welcoming settings. Done this way, the layout of the spaces responds to a lineal schematic and is sequential in nature. The central passage connects all the salons: the ivy-covered wall at the garden's end can be seen from the entrance.

Both the furnishings, the finishes and the lighting are similar throughout all of the salons. Decoration is almost non-existent: the architects have exclusively taken as a base reference the materials and lighting to create a tranquil, elegant atmosphere. Okoume wood

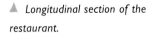 *Longitudinal section of the restaurant.*

▶ *Detail of one of the tables. The table lamp designed by Pep Anglí provides both warm ligting and intimate atmosphere.*

In the final room the side walls as well as the roof and floor are panelled in wood. The flooring consists of Merbau floating parquet. (C1)

Detail of one of the tables. Dinner next to the ivy-covered wall is one of the main attractions of the Gaig restaurant.

veneered board facing along the wall's entire length separating the restaurant from the kitchen and stores and on the patio roof, the opposing wall has been whitewashed, the ceiling stuccoed in yellow and the floor laid with Merbau floating parquet in all of the restaurant's salons. These finishes give the restaurant a warm ambience, yellows and reddish browns, accentuated by the lighting from the screen lights situated on each of the tables.

The garden constitutes a reference point not only for the last salon, but also for the entire restaurant. The ivy-covered walls constitute the chromatic counterpoint for the wood-covered surfaces. The architects have left an empty space between the garden's adobe wall and one of the glass side partitions where the climbing plants grow right next to the restaurant's tables. Everything has changed, but the most attractive corner is still to be found in the same place. ■

▲ *Next to the garden wall, two rows of lights are seen. the table lamps and the row of dicroic lights fixed to the wall.*

▼ *Detail of the tables of this room. The window is located just beside the garden wall. At night-time, the dark surface of the wall, just behind the glass, turns the window into a mirror.*

▼ *General view of the extension.*
The structure of this room is completely
new which has allowed the construction
of the sloping roof. The architects have
managed to give this space a look of
lightness. (C2)

Kristian Gavoille

▲ Detail of the entrance to the Cafe
Gavoille, which takes its name from
the architect who designed it.

▶ Night-time view from the
square located just in front of the restaurant.

Through the large windows giving onto the square, the scenes at night from the intensely lit interior inside the cafetería are projected out towards the street. The exterior appearance of the Gavoille café is reminiscent of the painting by Edward Hooper: The Nighthawkers; it is a sentimental landscape on the other side of the enormous glass windows, the artificial colouring bursts forth into the calm night, but the lighting does not manage to hide a certain depth which moistens everything, it only breaks the darkness like the sound of a trumpet.

Kristian Gavoille, the architect, explains that the atmosphere of the restaurant tries to pay homage to the world of the theatre and cinema. The cafeteria-restaurant is located in La Maison de la Culture in the French town of Amiens, in a remodelled building dating from the sixties.

"Like an advert in the street
I have wanted it.
The decoration, borrowed from the

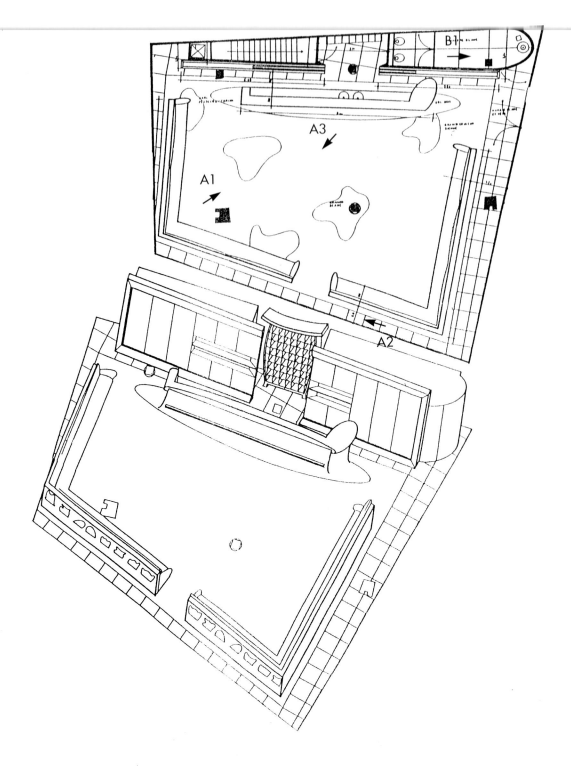

A3

A1

A2

B-1

▲ Floor plan and axonometry.

▶ The cafeteria-restaurant is located in
the Maison de la Culture in the French
city of Amiens, a building of the sixties
which has been recently remodelled.

vocabulary of the theatre and cinema.
borrowed from la Maison de la Culture
our home."

As explained by Kristian Gavoille, the
chandeliers are a tribute paid to the theatre.
They are not lights which illuminate, but are
illuminated instead. Hung from the ceiling,
where the original building's wrought-ironwork
structure has been left visible, the chandeliers,
in conjunction with the enormous luminous
shaded screen behind the bar, seem to form

▲ *General view of the restaurant.*
The appearance of the restaurant
changes completely from daytime to
night-time due to natural and artificial
lighting, which create a range of
different chromatic effects. (A1)

OUI OU

part of some half-abandoned scene from another place. Behind the benches, the circulation signs figure, inspired in the show halls from the turn of the century.

An orange sanded glass shaded screen installed behind the bar on the wall forming the back of the premises, extends from one end of the wall to the other: measuring 14 m long and 2.50 m high. The luminous screen is inspired by the cinema screens. In this case, no image is projected onto it, the scene takes places immediately in front of it, in the bar

▼ View of the room with the screen in the background. Kristian Gavoille has used influences from the world of theatre and cinema in the design of the premises. The screen just behind the bar brings to mind the silver screen of the cinema.

▲ Detail of the continuous bench that goes round the room just in front of the glass facade. The way the bench surrounds the room marks out the limits of the restaurant with respect to the square more than the glass facade. (A2)

◄ Elements from different periods have been combined in the Gavoille. The hanging lamps pay homage to the world of theatre. The ceiling shows the original construction of the building with its concrete structure. The furniture, however, introduces present tendencies in industrial design. (A3)

at, to observe the street from the cafeteria and vice versa.

But this is not all, the elements belonging to the different settings, facing one another, out of place, the new set against the old, the luminous against the opaque, all the objects can be seen. ■

◄ *Detail of the wine rack that is situated just behind the bar. Kristian Gavoille has been influenced by the shape of oriental pagodas.*

▼ *Detail of one of the stools designed by Kristian Gavoille, who also collaborated for five years with the French designer Philippe Starck.*

itself. This converts anyone standing in front of the screen into a protagonist. This taste for the scenographic, the constant references to the cinema, comes close to the architecture of Philippe Starck, with whom Kristian Gavoille worked for five years from 1986 to 1991, prior to setting up his own studio.

"The incredibly long bar has been valued, it appears to come right up out of the floor.

Like in work of Cocteau, it goes through the screen to reach the bottle rack."

In effect, as explained by Gavoille, the only element that interrupts the luminous stretch is a pagoda-shaped bottle rack - 2.70 m high and 2.30 m wide-. The light is reflected through the bottles against the stainless steel back.

However, beyond the more obvious details, of the hints continually left by the architect, there is an essential concept of the cinema and theatre which is found in the conceptual origin of this restaurant: voyeurism. Everything in the Gavoille is designed to look at and be looked

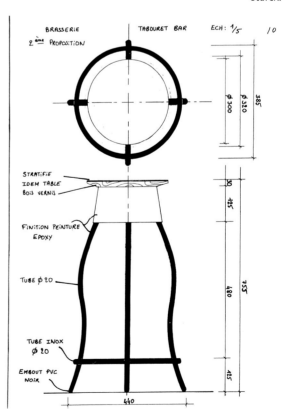

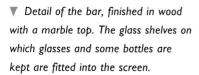
One of the ends of the bar finishes in a geometrical volute, the other in a circular table which favours the relationship between those who sit down to have a drink here.

▼ Detail of the bar, finished in wood with a marble top. The glass shelves on which glasses and some bottles are kept are fitted into the screen.

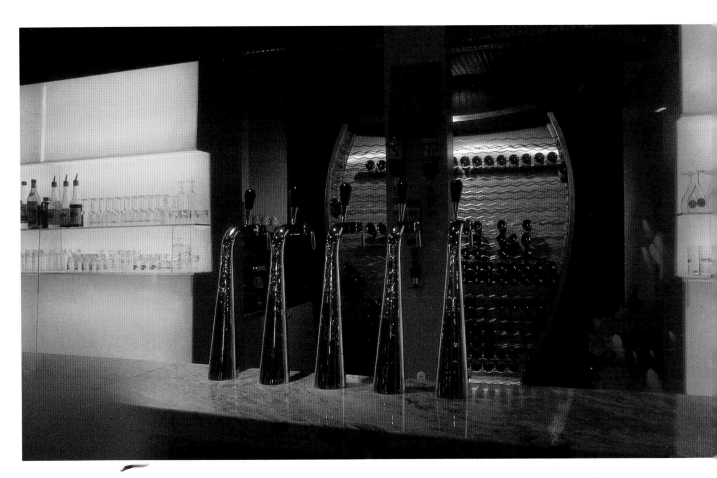

▲ *View of the washroom. This space has the same importance as the rest of the premises for the architect. An effort has been made to procure an image that is both singular and original.*

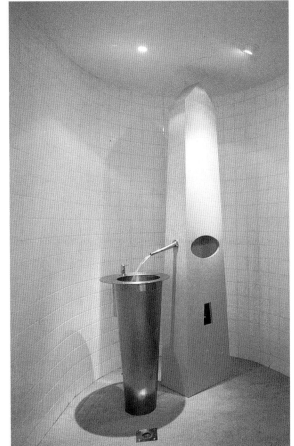

▶ *Detail of the chrome-plated beer taps. Just behind is the wine rack.*

THE PEOPLES PALACE

Allies and Morrison Architects

▲ *The Peoples Palace is sited on one
of the floors of the Royal Festival Hall.
Within the process of renovation of
this fifties building carried out in recent
years, Allies and Morrison were
entrusted with the design of the new*

▶ *Shot of the entrance. In the foreground,
the cloakroom door outlined on the wall which
separates the restaurant from the
kitchen can be seen.*

▲ General view of the Peoples Palace
from the stairway leading from the
Royal Festival Hall's vestibule to
the auditorium. To one side one of the
installations organised by the Arts
Council of Great Britain can be seen, on
the other side, the kitchen's wood-
panelled wall. (B1)

◄ Perspective of the entrance, where
the bridge leading up to the restaurant
entrance can be seen.

► The bar is found situated
between the restaurant's two
symmetrical entrances. Next to it, a
small raiesed wooden platform where
some tables have been placed directly
linked to the bar. (A1)

► General floor plan.

The Royal Festival Hall was built during the years 1949-50 as part of an extensive exhibition held then, which was subsequently called the Festival of Britain. Almost all of the buildings constructed for the event, situated between Waterloo Station and the river Thames, were later dismantled, only the Royal Festival Hall was left standing as a permanent reference to that exhibition.

The building was extended in 1964. New exhibition galleries were added on the river side, together with a restaurant and corridors for circulation, while on the other side, some offices were converted for the administration of the building.

Later on, in 1968, in the area surrounding the building, new auditories were installed: the Queen Elizabeth Hall and the Purcell Room and a gallery for artistic exhibitions: the Hayward. Access to all of these buildings was gained by the same elevated passages surrounding the Royal Festival Hall.

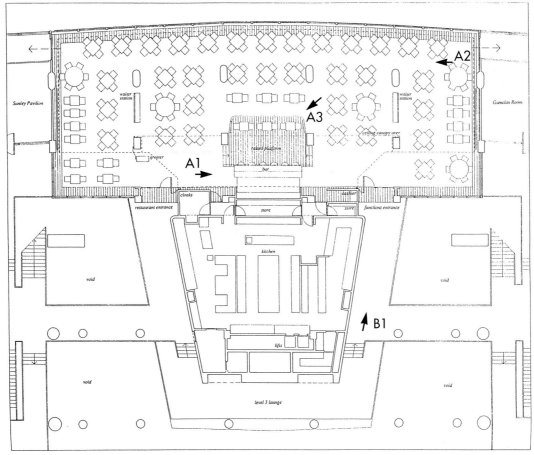

With the coming of the National Lottery, designed to collect funds to guarantee the development of the most important public projects, the possibility arose of being able to renovate the cultural complex in its entirety, including the restoration of the façades and the interior of the Royal Festival Hall. At the same time, the Royal Festival Hall then went on to form part of the list of buildings catalogued as Grade I, which meant the legal provision of public funds to prevent its deterioration.

The South Bank Centre began numerous improvements inside, including the restoration of the original constructions, and, in this

▲ *General view of the salon, showing the enormous columns supporting the auditorium. The large window in the façade offers a panoramic view out over the river Thames. (A2)*

▶ *Shot of the wall built by Allies and Morrison which is doubled and creates an interior cover. This structure of this false ceiling is independent of the structure of the auditorium.*

▶ *Light coloured wood, white painted surfaces and the large windows surrounding the entire restaurant create a warm setting of gentle hues and great lightness. (A3)*

▼ *Perspective of the interior.*

context, the designing of the new spaces starting in 1991 was proposed to Allies and Morrison.

One of the most complex projects consisted in remodelling the restaurant which had gone bankrupt and closed its doors in 1992. It was necessary to attract a partner who would direct the project and take charge of running it. In the end, the Capitals Hotel Group took over the restaurant.

The Peoples Palace, completed in 1995, is located on an intermediate floor which runs right along the façade of the building overlooking the Thames. It can hold up to 240 people, 20 places of which correspond to the bar and the elevated central platform.

The two main stairways which take the public from the auditorium up to the foyers found on the ground floor, go round both sides of the restaurant. The perimetral glass partitions allow the concert goers an untrammelled panoramic view of the triple

103

height grand hall with the river Thames in the background. The restaurant entrance is found via both passages or bridges on both sides.

Thelayout of the hall is organised around a slightly elevated central platform, next to the bar in the central zone, looking out over the river. The bar is situated next to a double-height wall which separates the restaurant salon from the kitchen.

The architects have tried to distinguish the new elements from the existing construction.

▲ *The architects wanted to differentiate between the new installation and the pre-existing structure. To this end, they have designed a series of outlines on the new wall which express this overlapping.*

To this end, they have outlined some brightly coloured boxes on the wall around the wooden doors communicating the salon with the kitchen, the cloakroom and the stores, which contrast with the whiteness of the wall.

On both sides of the restaurant, intense red curtains have been fitted with the aim of delimiting the space and the large glass frieze which looks out over the river. It is currently being used as a backdrop for the installations organised by the Arts Council of Great Britain. ▪

▲ *General view of the establishment at a busy moment. In the background, some concert goers can be seen looking into the restaurant from one of the walkways giving access to the auditorium.*

Mohamed Salahuddin Consulting Engineering Bureau
S.B. Karpe

▲ The Mexican fast food restaurant, Taco Maker in Bahrain combines the the aesthetics of a Persian Gulf country with references to Mexican culture, and communal elements from the consumer society culture.

▶ General view of the façade of the Taco Maker restaurant. The towers, one on each end, flank an arched centre with a wing of tiles.

Taco Maker is a Mexican fast food restaurant. It is located on an island in the Gulf of Persia, Bahrain. The peripheral context, close to a motorway with no other reference, could be that of anywhere.

The project was developed as a one-storey building. The flat roof is accessible. The parapet running along it defines a horizontal strip on the four façades which is used as a hoarding. The body of the main façade, formed by five arches, is flanked by the two square double-height towers which crown the entrances. A wing of ceramic tiles separates the arches from the parapet.

The building auto-proclaims itself. Elements of traditional Mexican architecture are reiterated in the restaurant. Its walls are stuccoed and painted. By day, colours appear, in the form of tiling and metalwork on the luminous texture and neutral glass structure of the building. It is only at night, however, when the building really becomes a advert in its own right.

▲ *Shot of one of the towers. The top parapet is used as an advertising hoarding. The restaurant is found in a setting with scarcely any other references.*

► *Plans of the main facade and the back of the buildings.*

► *Longitudinal and transversal section in which the skylights that illuminate the interior are seen.*

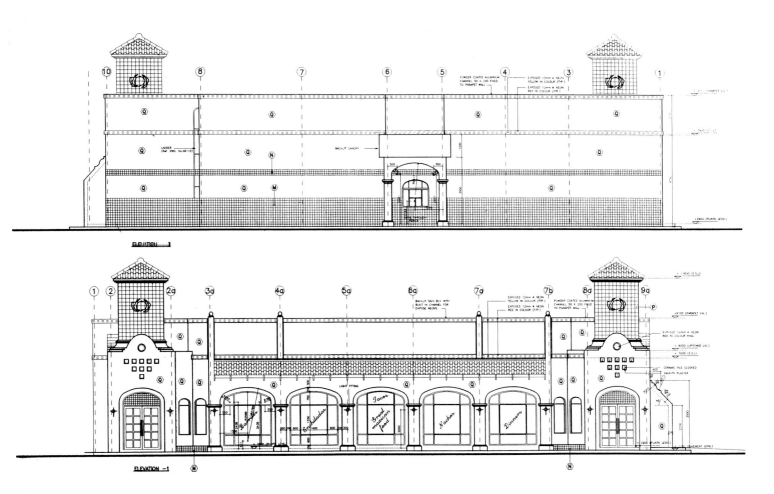

ELEVATION

ELEVATION - 1

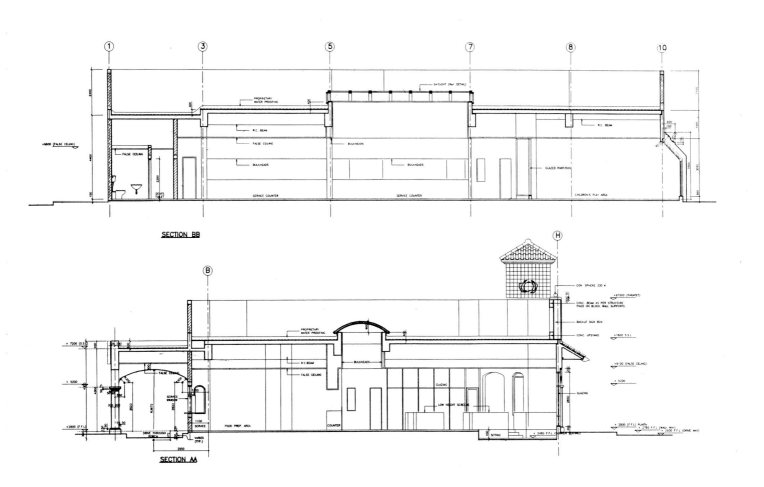

SECTION BB

SECTION AA

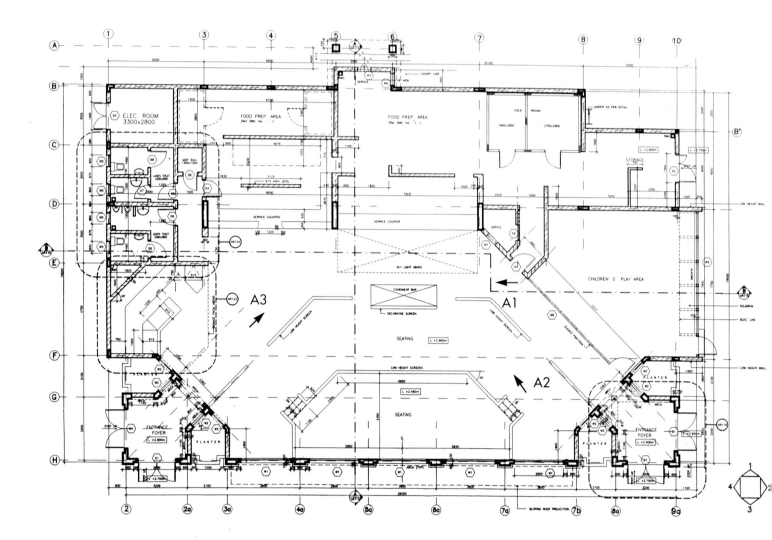

An exterior image designed to attract is the intention. The combination of bright, warm colours with different textures make it so: red, orange and yellow point up the white, drawing an arrow over the entrance doors; forming mosaic bands on the walls; and covering the towers entirely.

The building, roughly rectangular in shape, can be driven around. In fact, on the rear façade, a section of the porch on columns allows cars to stop next to the fast service takeaway window. The rest of the façade, totally blind, corresponds to the services area (stores, cold-storage rooms, kitchen and installations area) and one corner is used to support the hand stairs leading up to the roof.

As in other MSCEB projects, like the Jawad commercial complex and the BATELCO offices (in Manama, Bahrain), the layout of Taco Maker is developed based on a 45° geometry. From

General floor plan of the restaurant.

110

the entrance towers on the corners, two diagonals lead to a central space, next to the counter, lit at the zenith through an elongated skylight. This run surrounds the seating area, resting on the two wall strips that repeat the same movement. The play area for children is sited next to the right-hand diagonal, a space between windows, linked with the outside.

At night, the building is transformed into a pure visual effect, into a neon advertisement. Camouflaged during the daytime, the neon lights burst forth into the darkness: they run right around the parapet, brightly lighting up the advertising hoarding, highlighting in red the lines of the arches and the restaurant's logotype on the top of the towers too.

The project harks back to the North American "strip", bringing to mind the book by Venturi *Learning from Las Vegas*, as a source of inspiration; the architecture wants to get close to the user and, to this end, gets the most out of the advertisements' communicative capacity.

The brightly lit interior reaches out through the arches: new neon lights, false a false ceiling of diagonal lines, tiles and coloured furnishings... ▨

▼ *General night-time view. At night, the restaurant's appearance changes dramatically. The building becomes a construction of neon lights.*

▲ View of the main façade at night. In the darkness, with the intense colouring of the neon advertisements, Taco Maker acquires all of its strength and vitality.

▶ General view of the interior, where the food serving counter can be seen. The open zenith skylight over this area can also be seen. (A1)

▲ *View of the table area. The design of the interior is governed by the same aesthetic criteria as the outside. Once again, luminous advertisements and intense colours are used. (A2)*

▼ *The inside is designed as a single, large unitary space, where the different settings are configured by the distribution of the furnishings themselves. (A3)*

ASO-KUJU NATIONAL PARK RESTAURANT

Masaharu Takasaki

▲ The restaurant is situated in the Asu-Kuju national park which occupies the area between the Asu and Kuju mountains. For this reason, the design of the building had to be adapted to the numerous restrictions imposed by the Environmental Agency.

▶ View of the building entrance with the stairway giving access to the first floor in the background. Colour usage was one of the primary considerations, with the aim of achieving a chromatic range that reflected the different intensities of sunlight and seasonal changes. (AI)

The restaurant designed by Masaharu Takasaki is sited in a privileged location indeed. At 1,100 m altitude, alone on the mountainside, surrounded by the exuberant countryside of the Asu-Kuju national park.

Takasaki was always aware, right from the very first moment, that the restaurant was going to become the sole architectonic reference point in the territory. Thus, rather than the building adapting itself to the countryside, it had to endeavour to express the extraordinary impression of Man against nature.

▲ General exterior view. Concrete, the material used in constructing virtually all of the building's component parts, provided the architect with a great degree of formal freedom, enabling him to design extraordinarily long windows and large projections.

▲ Masaharu Takasaki built a series of elements which flow from the inside out and vice versa, with the aim of connecting the building with the forms of the countryside and the passage of the sun.

Masaharu Takasaki's buildings all have a particular hallmark. Peter Cook of Archigram, the group which in the sixties and seventies contributed some of the most innovative, radical visions that have managed to make architecture come alive, when he was a judge at the competition in which Takasaki presented his work just after graduating stated: "I am terrified by this work."

Indeed, the architecture of Masaharu Takasaki is filled with surprising forms. His

projects have a highly uncommon origin: architecture is taken right to the limits of present day knowledge, almost indescribable. He himself has said that "I would like to direct the voices of the primitive, of nature, of humanity and the divine, as a starting point for shaping the design of the spaces to those existing on the Earth."

The character of the Asu-Kuju restaurant is cosmological. It is a building designed to experience the emotion of nature. Not only by its close presence and beauty, but also by its existence in relation to night and day, its capacity to evoke the passage of time, to relate the reciprocal movement of the stars and the Earth's trajectory through the Universe. It is a building constructed to capture the infinite changes of light and colour which take place in nature itself, in walls, in the sky, at all times of day and in every season. Hence, the building, rather than the topography or the views, is designed in relation to the passage of the sun,

▲ *Image of the restaurant at dusk.
"Architecture must recreate our
relationship with spiritual things"
states Takasaki.*

117

▲ General shot of the stairway built in the centre of the building. The restaurant rooms are located on the first floor, making it necessary to go up the stairway from the ground floor. f9: Detail of one of the terraces. The building is completely open to the exterior. Only the kitchen and some of the restaurant rooms are closed in with glass facings. The central stairway is totally exterior. (B1)

▶ Nocturnal view of the building. The illumination is not homogenously produced, but is instead projected night-wards trying to produce a particular combination of different colours.

▶ The building is not lit from the outside, all of the lighting comes from inside. The light coming through the elongated windows is reminiscent of the twinkling of shooting stars and starshine.

◄ *Detail of one of the terraces. The building is completely open to the exterior. (B2)*

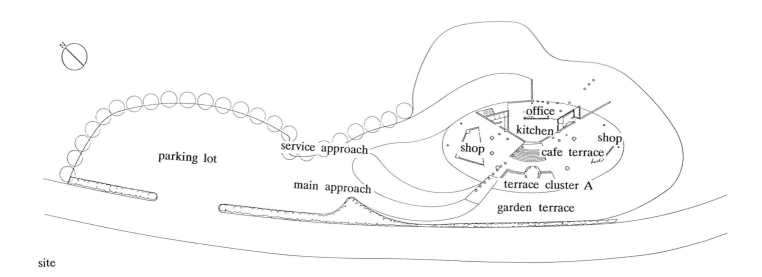

site

▲ *General floor plan of the siting.*

the changes of light and the shadows cast by the different elements of its architecture. The building designed by Asu-Kuju, like the megalithic monument of Stonehenge, thus has a cosmological character.

"I particularly made an effort to create a fluid exterior, in designing a chromatic layout inside and how to move the visitors up to the upper floors of the restaurant in as careful a manner as possible, ensuring that they received an ambience full of sensations and feelings": Masaharu Takasaki sums up in this phrase the most important design lines used to achieve that communion between the building and nature, and to transmit that emotivity to the visitor. The shapes which flow from the inside out and vice versa, connect the architecture

► *Ground floor plan.*

► *First floor plan.*

► *Second floor plan.*

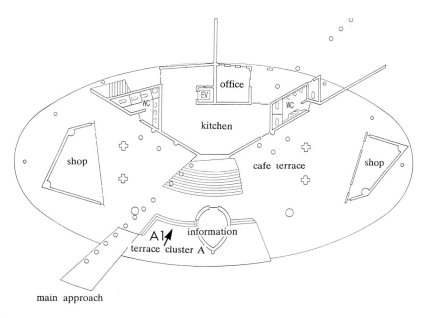

first level

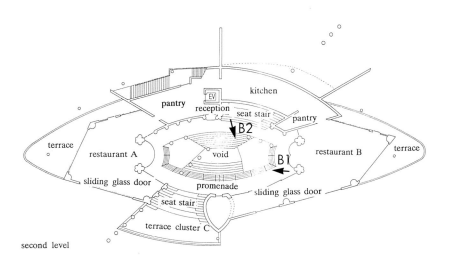

second level

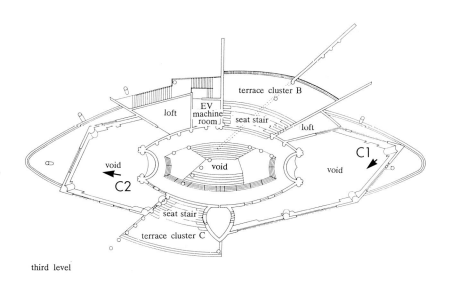

third level

▲ Overhead view of the stairway. It does bear a certain resemblance to a primitive temple, thereby imbuing it with something approaching a spiritual air.

▶ Section of the restaurant.

▶ General view of one of the rooms of the restaurant. furnishing is minimal. There is a deliberate movement between the function of the building and its scale. The interior colours range from blue to purple. (C1)

▶ Detail of the central stairway's giant columns. Passage up stairs takes on a ceremonial nature. The architect tries to transmit an atmosphere of sensations and feelings to those arriving at the restaurant.

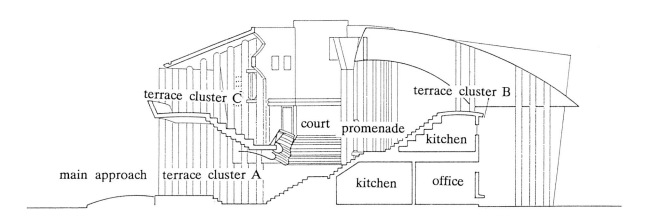

main approach   terrace cluster A   terrace cluster C   court   promenade   kitchen   terrace cluster B   kitchen   office

with the profiles of the Asu and Kuju mountains. For Takasaki, joining interior and exterior does not consist of opening up large windows but instead, in modifying the architecture in relation to the form of the countryside, moving the walls, allowing the mountain to invade the building, constructing a rhythm via the architectonic elements which have as their counterpoint the territorial elements and the movement of the stars.

As the architect himself has remarked, an essential part of that rhythm arises from the building's chromatic graduation. A range of colours which go from blue through to purple, trying to reflect some of the sites' most surprising chromatic variations. Each season establishes a different relationship with the building.

The different rooms of the restaurant are located on the top floor, distributed all along the façade. The floor plan of the building is spindle-shaped, with the centre being empty. The reception is located on the ground floor, together with a café, a couple of small shops and the kitchen. To get to the restaurant rooms, one has to ascend via a grand central flight of stairs. This ascension takes on a ceremonial nature. The stairway is monumental, with enormous columns, some of them open, dominating a theatrical space, open to the sky, as if it were a temple from a lost civilisation. The furnishings in the restaurant are minimal. The ceiling and the walls are built using concrete. It could be thought that the tables have been casually placed, more to take advantage of the available space or to provide some functionality, but is instead an extension of the surrounding countryside itself. ▪

▲ *"Architecture, which forces the study of the existence of human beings in its entirety and which is an independent, vital landscape object in its own right, must carry us with it between the universe of animals, plants and nature."*

HOTEL MARTINSPARK

Dietmar Eberle & Karl Baumschlager

Shot of the main entrance. The restaurant is found on the first floor. The entrance is located just below it.(A1)

The restaurant's volume stands out over the plain façade of the hotel. Its shape is somewhat similar to the prow of a ship. The architects have accentuated the contrast

The Martinspark Hotel is integrated in a newly built complex in the centre of Dornbirn Vorarlberg in Austria.

This is a hotel for businessmen spending one or two days in the town. Rectangularly floored, the rooms are distributed around the central well. The hotel's appearance is characterised by the treatment given to the façade, based around blue screened sliding shutters. The blue panels slide over the glass windows on each of the floors, thereby creating a mobile mosaic.

Over this sober gridlike structure, on the west façade, a large volume of oxidised copper strongly stands out: the restaurant. Warped shapes and green surfaces, the restaurant

▲ *General view of the west façade, with the notable volume of the restaurant which appears to be suspended in mid-air, an effect due to the slendar metal pillars which support in being hidden in shadow.*

▶ *General siting plan. The hotel's footprint is rectangular based around a central well. The restaurant is the only element which juts out from the square perimeter.*

▶ *View of the restaurant's exterior facings. The narrow, elongated windows coincide with the joins between the green-coloured pre-oxidised copper sheeting.*

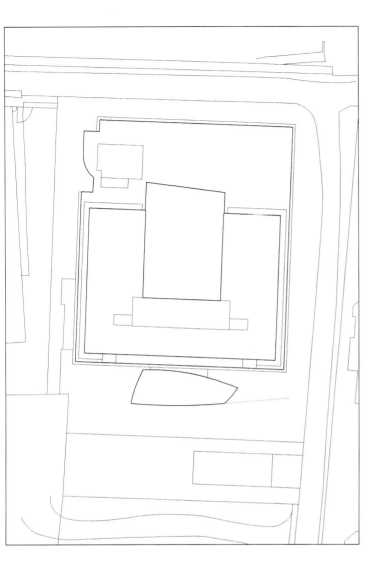

appears to sail at a snail's pace, suspended in the air, like the hull of a ship washed up on the shore after a shipwreck, or like a dirigible balloon about to launch into flight over the town. It is hung from slender metal pillars. The windows are elongated, narrow slits, opening at different heights, which coincide with the longitudinal lines of the joins between the copper sheeting.

The hotel entrance is located below the volume of the restaurant. In this way, the only piece standing out on the planes of the façades signals entrance to the building and, at the same time, fulfils the same function as the traditional canopies or porches at hotel exits.

In the vestibule, over the hotel's rectangular geometry, a double-height elliptical space has been outlined of approximately the same exterior volume as the restaurant. Hence, producing a curious anti-symmetry. The piece that appears to be suspended in front of the façade, with an independent logic to the rest of the building, corresponds to the empty space produced inside. What appears to be a mystery from the square, reveals its identity on entering the hotel.

ANSICHT OSTEN   1:500

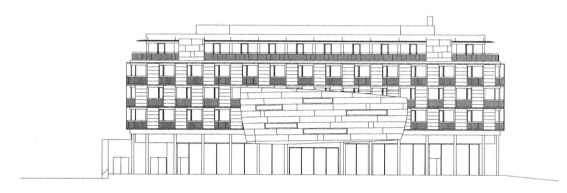

ANSICHT WESTEN   1:500

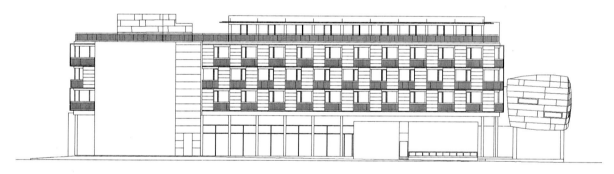

ANSICHT NORDEN   1:500

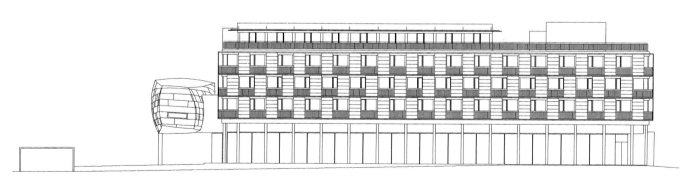

ANSICHT SÜDEN   1:500

What is more, after going up the stairs leading through the double space up to the first floor, we find that the restaurant setting not only circumscribes the exterior volume, but also occupies its projection out to the other side of the façade. The exterior salon corresponds to the restaurant's main salon, where the tables are located, but around the double elliptical space other functions connected to the restaurant are organised, such as the cafetería and kitchen, which is installed in a contiguous area.

The restaurant's interior is based around great simplicity, Baumschlager and Eberle have done away with decorative elements, with the idea being that the diners can have an untrammelled view of the the singular shape of the spaces. Only the narrow, elongated windows permit the entry into the salon of strips of landscape and rays of light which sketch the illuminated profile of the openings

◀ *Plan of the different elevations of the hotel and restaurant.*

▲ *General night-time view. The relationship between the volumes of the hotel and restaurant change totally, owing to the lighting of the rooms.*

131

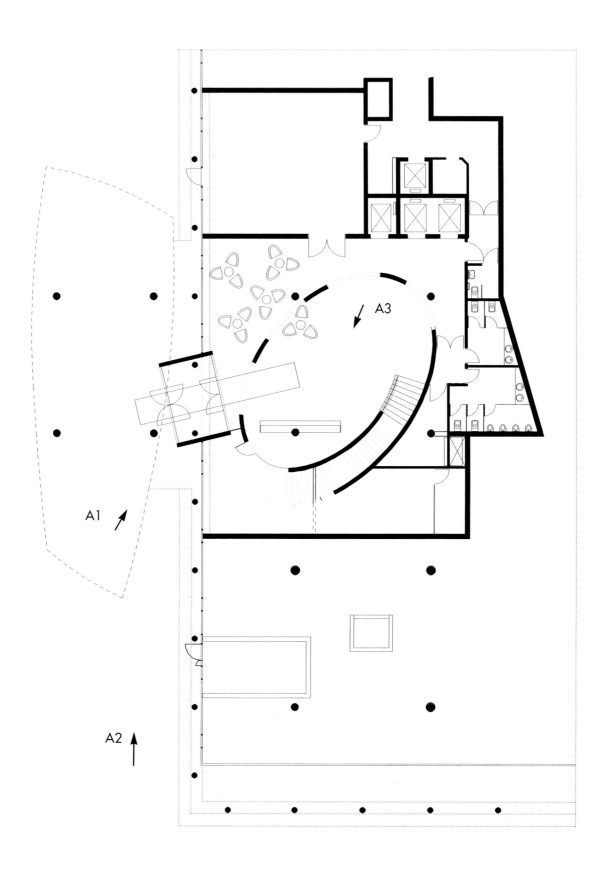

▼ *Plan of the vestibule detail on the ground floor. (A1)*

A3

A1

A2

▼ *General view of the vestibule, with the entrance door in the background. The double space is elliptically shaped. The bar can be found in the upper section. (A3)*

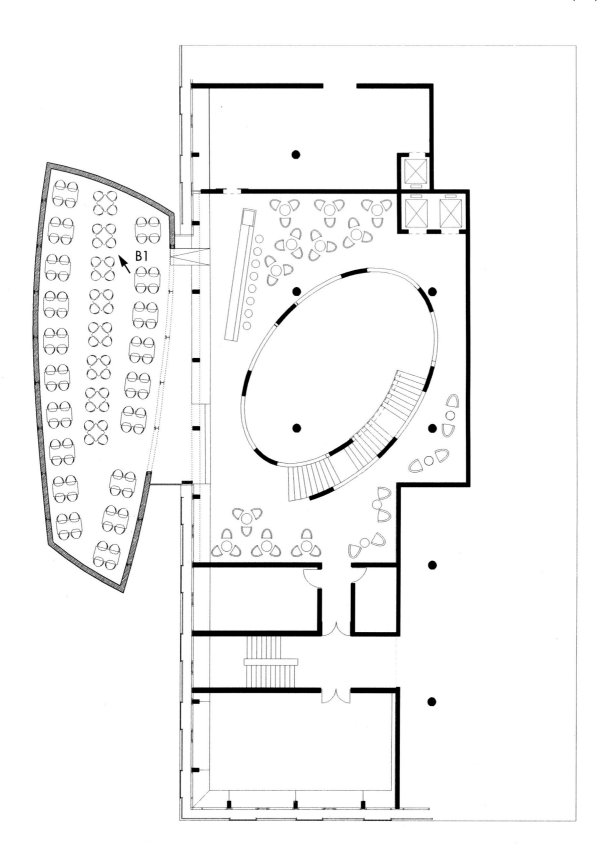

B1

on the opposing walls. The windows have not been build at eye level, but are instead cut off at different heights with no direct relationship to the tables.

Owing to its rather unusual form and the distribution of the windows, the restaurant salon, in addition to fulfilling its specific role, also constitutes a space with an intrinsic architectonic value, a space conceived to provoke sensations, to be experienced. ■

▲ *General view of the restaurant salon. There are no decorative elements. The flooring is parquet and the walls are plastered and painted white. The narrow, elongated windows throw rays of light, especially in the late afternoon, onto the opposing walls where they are reflected. (B1)*

135

One of the side walls displays the flamboyant symbol of Belgo Centraal, together with the date of opening, Spring, 1995.

This dining-room represents a good example of the search for new forms, a characteristic trait of Arad and his work.

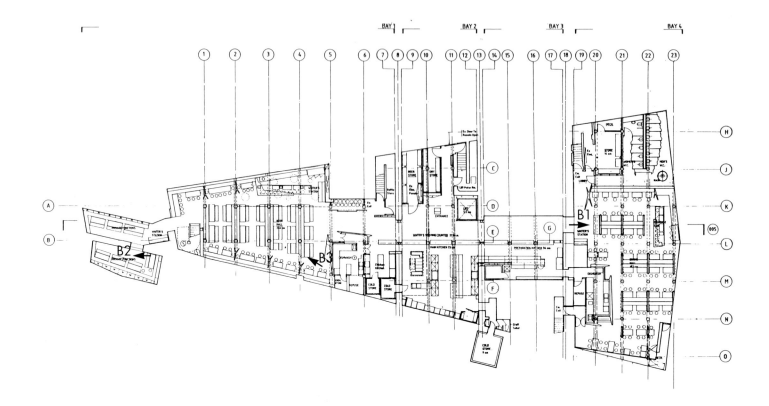

"One of the most interesting and suggestive phenomena in British design in the last decade." Definitions such as this are used to describe Ron Arad, born in Tel Aviv in 1951 and resident in London since he started his studies at the Architectural Association School of Architecture in 1973. His first professional moves were in the direction of architectural work in London, until he started up the legendary furniture showroom and sales outlet One Off, in 1981.. This specific project, finished in April 1995, turned the gleaming hub of the restaurant – the kitchen – into a spectacle of space, light, machinery, and activity.

The nineteenth-century building, originally a warehouse has been transformed into a prism bisected by an entrance area with three storerooms. On the restaurant level, a smooth, lustrous counter stretches along one third of the 65 yards of the avenue, separating the open space of the kitchen from the customers and visually connecting two 200-seat dining areas. Each of these dining areas has a bar 40 feet long serving Belgian beer from fully visible casks alongside sliding mesh panels.

The experience begins outside the restaurant; the kitchen is a public place, visible from the 20-foot-high glazed entrance facade. "Every slice of every mushroom in full view," explains its architect, Alison Brooks.

The sturdy elevator is brilliantly lit and as it moves, its mesh cladding creates a slow-motion kinetic silhouette in conjunction with the

▲ *Basement of the building.*

▶ *Under the direction of Ron Arad Associates, the old nineteenth century beer cellar has become one of the most frequented places of the city centre of London.*

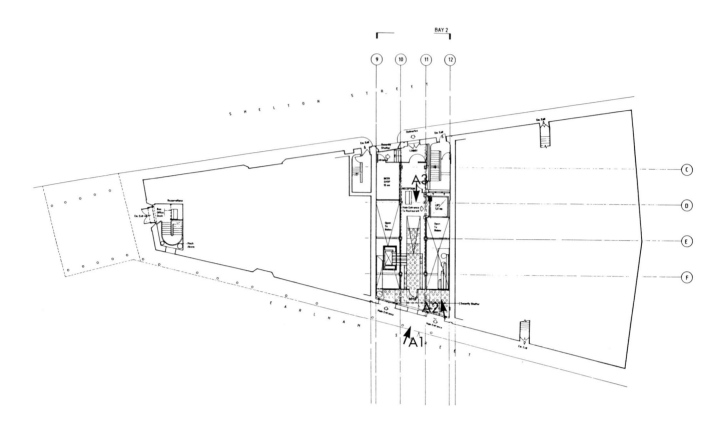

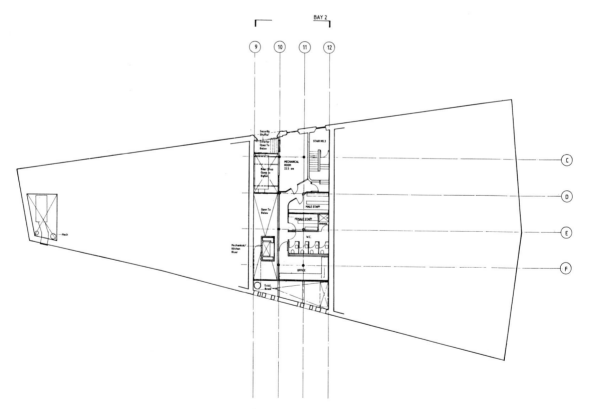

movement of the customers as they walk in. The kitchen top, 70 feet long, displays its huge stock of plates, pots, and pans, as if it were a showcase for cut glass; this luminous horizontal surface leads to the two vaulted dining areas, where the shiny bulges of the boilers conceal the modest dishwashers.

"Mountains" of spiral aluminum sheeting connect the long benches in the beer hall and separate the back part of this from the dining

▲ *General view of the main entrance, with the walls painted in red. (AI)*

◀ *On the previous page, general floor plan of the mezzanine, where the design of the entrance, the bridge that crosses the space and the doorways to the lower floor can be seen.*

◀ *On the previous page, the first floor.*

◀ *Detail of one of the entrance arches to the premises. The interior bridge which crosses the space can be seen. (A2)*

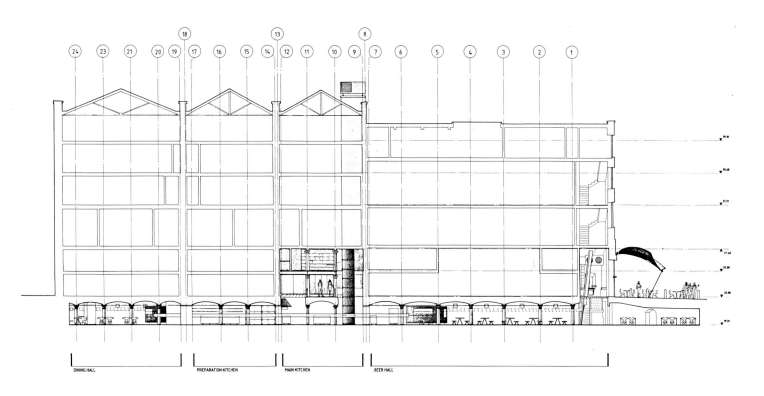

| DINING HALL | PREPARATION KITCHEN | MAIN KITCHEN | BEER HALL |

◀ Interior view of the entrance with the long bridge crossing the space. To the left of the photo the open kitchen can be seen. (A3)

◀ The imposing industrial lift leads customers to the different dining-rooms.

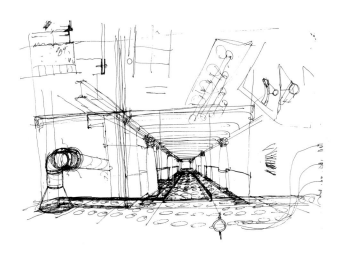

▲ General view of one of the main dining-rooms. The combination of wood and steel lit by a careful array of lights is one of the main attractions of Belgo Centraal. (B1)

► *Private dining-room in one of the old beer cellars. The new furniture within the ancient space originates an original encounter. (B2)*

▼ *The geometrical lay-out of a few elements, such as menus placed on the tables, gives special movement to the premises. (B3)*

▼ *Sketches of the design of the benches and tables in one of the restaurants.*

area, while the side of the restaurant has individual alcoves with stools for customers who prefer a quieter atmosphere. These alcoves are set against a glass partition and shed light from the gaps in the galvanized spiral decoration.

The first unisex toilets in London, complete with communal hand-washing facilities, are located in an independent structure in crimped aluminum.

◀ *Detail of the aluminium benches in one of the dining-rooms.*

▼ *General floor plan of the main floor of Belgo Centraal, located at 50, Earlham Street.*

it which is on the exterior acting primarily as a sun screen. The original plan was for all the boards to be in wood, but the need for easy maintenance and general durability convinced the designers to make the boarding out of wood only on the inside of the building; on the exterior, above the glass roof, it switches to steel. Both the wood and the steel display large circular holes which "bear witness to the form of the construction without detracting from its purpose as a device for providing protection from the sun."

The solution adopted for the roof of the restaurant is especially interesting. Projecting a successful restaurant in a confined space with limited access poses particular problems for designers and builders alike. For the structural engineers of the project, this consideration "explains how some of the problems were solved, how the structural design developed, and at the same time gives detailed information about some key structural elements." Being a warehouse, the original intention in the form given to this century-old building was to restrict the entry of natural light. Given these circumstances, it was decided that daylight should enter through the roof, and that the new roof should drain onto the existing one.

It was from this starting point that the concept governing the structure of the roof was developed: an inclined plane of glass expressed in slices through a series of molded boards with a depth ratio of 4 to 1. The boarding traverses the glass roof, that part of

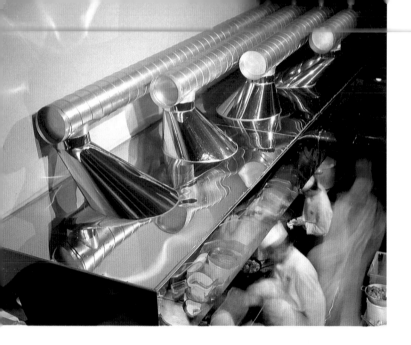

▲ The "engine' of the restaurant, the kitchen, forms part of the spectacle of space, light, machinery and action. The "open plan" kitchen breaks one of the great traditions of a restaurant of "prestige".

▼ ► The glass roof lets natural light through. The beams (made of wood in the interior and steel in the exterior) form protection and adapt to the unitary form of the space.

The outer walls, which are painted bright red at the level of the entrance, the original design of the chairs and tables (Arad in his designer role), the recurring steel complements arranged at intervals throughout the interior, the decorative elements with their loud forms; all these are inherent features of Ron Arad's rebellious, aggressive firm.

This work, like all of Arad's, is the outcome of his unique approach to the creative process which, although it is undoubtedly in the mainstream of contemporary trends, at the same time avoids stereotypes. Arad transgresses conventions, and his search for beauty through new forms endows his work with a special elegance, beyond the norm. His quest for beauty in our day-to-day environment, in this case a restaurant, gives the most commonplace reality a high degree of aesthetic dignity. ■

▲ The Little Italy restaurant has a
profound exterior leaning. It is sited on
a terrace overlooking the port of
Barcelona and the city's maritime
façade. Access is gained via the terrace
itself, where other bars and restaurants
are also located. Top, shot of the
lattice separating this establishment
from the one next door.

▶ General view of the terrace of Little
Italy. The restaurant is sited in the new
leisure-commercial centre of Barcelona,
located in the city's old industrial port area.

The Little Italy restaurant is situated in one of the more recently built leisure spaces in the city of Barcelona. Like many other port cities, in recent years Barcelona has carried out a reconversion process of its industrial port, transforming it into a leisure and consumer zone. The cranes, silos and containers have been moved to another part of the coast, further out from the city's urban centre, and the old maritime installations have been renovated or demolished to make way for the construction of shopping malls, restaurants and cinemas.

One of the most ambitious projects, the Maremagnum complex, sited on a dock right at the end of the popular tourist boulevard, Las Ramblas, was handled by the architects Albert Viaplana and Helio Pinón. Their project extended the urban boulevard via a wooden walkway extending out over the port,

terminating in a two-storey building, with
terraces open to the city's port maritime
façade. The Little Italy restaurant, designed by
Pilar Líbano, is sited on the second floor of
this building. This establishment therefore has
a double origin and scale. Its first genesis
responds to a new city concept, to a revision
of historical sites, changing them from
production centres into leisure areas for
tourism, leisure and shopping. Its scale is that
of the city itself, or larger still, that of the

▲ *Detail of a corner of the terrace
at nighfall. The profile of the city made
out against the sunset.*

151

territory. The new buildings are designed to receive large crowds at night, weekends or in the summer, people coming from all over the region, or even from abroad. Hence, the spaces transmit a certain feeling of scale, extensive terraces where the bars, restaurants and shops follow on one from the other, pillars soaring several floors, enormous porches, stairways and windows visible from the other side of the docks, elements destined to shape the landscape.

Right after the urban scale comes the individual one. Each establishment unleashes its singularity, its difference toward the visitor, like the song of a siren.

Next to the walkways, the terraces and the docks, there coexists a universe in which the different establishments unfurl opposing irreconcilable finishes and aesthetics, stridently singular furnishings and scenographic ambiences. There is a certain intermediate scale which fades out between the maritime walkway and the anecdotal seat.

152

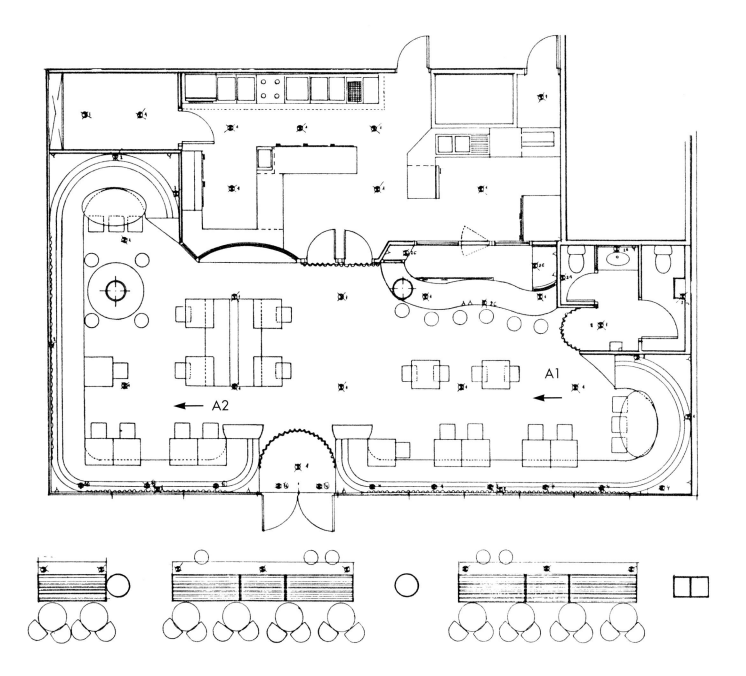

▲ Plan of the restaurant's general
floor layout.

◀ The restaurant ventures out into large-
dimensioned spaces: the port, the
maritime walkway, the outline of the city's
monuments, ... The terrace, the pillars
and porch all form part of this urban
scale, while the tables, chairs and the
remaining furnishings belong to the
individual scale.

◀ Shot of one of tables at Little Italy.
These have been designed especially for
this establishment. Made using teak with
a glass top under which maccaroni,
tortellini, spaghetti and other kinds of
pasta have been put as decorative
elements. The base is made of turned
teak.

153

Little Italy is a restaurant offering dishes from the different regions of Italy. The establishment is divided up into two settings: the terrace and the inside. Barcelona is a city blessed with a particularly benign climate, hence it is possible for many months during the year to enjoy leisure time out of doors, this being a prevalent tendency among its inhabitants. One of the attractions of the restaurants in the Maremagnum complex is their large terraces with views out over the port and the city. The decor there plays a relatively minor role in relation to their siting as compared to the views. Inside, on the other hand, an identifying image has to be found.

Pilar Líbano took her inspiration from American restaurants dating from the fifties: the era that saw the birth of Rock 'n' Roll and electrical home appliances. The designer brought back chrome finishes and synthetic fabrics when designing Little Italy to attract the slick-haired youth of today and modern housewives: loudly coloured skay chairs and

▲ *As opposed to the outside spaces, the interior is governed by much more delimited dimensions. (A1)*

▼ *One of the elements characterising the interior of Little Italy is a bench running right around the establishment's perimeter. (A2)*

▶ *Pilar Líbano took her inspiration from the aesthetics of the fifties. Nevertheless, the play of bright colours transfigures this rather forlorn image.*

154

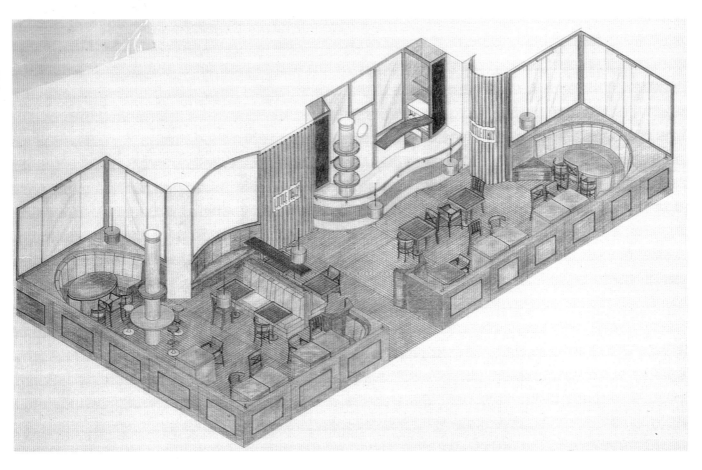

◄ *Shot of the bar, finished in chromed metal. The lights are drum model with green velvet shades. Wood has also been widely used throughout the whole restaurant: very dark African wood for the floor and teak for the furnishings.*

velvet shade lamps. The establishment was created with a premature decadence, the greater part of the chairs are different models, as if some had been already broken and had been replaced with mismatching chairs, taken from other places. Pilar Líbano is ironic about this new enthusiasm toward leisure culture which these monumental leisure complexes, shrines to mass culture, are trying to convey, recalling to memory the aesthetics of another era with the same imagination. ■

▲ *Axonometric shot of the establishment's interior.*

◄ *Pilar Líbano has introduced mismatched chairs into the establishment, odd models, which appear to have replaced in an offhand manner chairs previously broken. This gives the restaurant a prematurely decadent look.*

157

- Chicago, 1958
- Studies at the Art Institute of Chicago and after, at the University of Illinois, 1984.
- In 1984 Jordan Mozer & Associates Ltd. was founded in Chicago, in which 20 people worked.
- Some of his most important projects are the following: the factories Outer Circle's (1995) and H20 Plus in Chicago (1994), the restaurants Cheesecake Factory in Chicago (1995), New Wind in Frankfurt (1993), the Surf'n Turf in Matsuyama (1992) and the Cypress Club in San Francisco (1991).

▶ JOSEP LLUÍS GARCÍA

- Barcelona, 1953
- Studies at La Escuela Superior de Arquitectura de Barcelona, 1981.
- In 1990 his own office was founded in Barcelona.
- He has designed various shops for the Simorra chain in Barcelona and Madrid, the shop Trazos, the feline clinic Tot Cat, the Simorlinea offices and several detached houses in Barcelona.

▶ PHILIPPE STARCK

- Paris, 1949.
- Studies at Notre Dame de Sainte Croix de Neully and at the Ecole Nissim de Camonde de Paris.
- His work includes architecture; the Asahi and Nani Nani buildings in Tokyo, the Baron Vert building in Osaka and the National School of Decorative Arts in Paris, interior design; the Mondrian Hotel in Los Angeles, the Delano Hotel in Miami, the Paramount and Royalton Hotels in New York, the Groningen Museum and the restaurants Teatriz in Madrid and Cafe Mystique in Tokyo, industrial design; furniture for Kartell, Xo, mikli glasses, lamps for Flos, motorbikes for Aprilia,.....

▶ ALFREDO ARRIBAS

- Barcelona, 1954.
- Studies at the Escuela Superior de Arquitectura de Barcelona, 1977.

- In 1986 Alfredo Arribas Arquitectos Asociados (AAAA) with Miguel Morte is founded.
- The following works stand out among his projects; the Network Cafe in Barcelona, the space Crossing in Fukuoka, the Hirai Museum of Contemporary Spanish Art in Marugame or the show-room prototype for the new Mercedes car Smart and Swatch.

▶ ISMAELE MORRONE

- Cologno al Serio, 1954.
- Studies at the Instituto di Venezia, 1980.
- In 1983 his own studio was opened in Milan.
- Among his works are detached houses and apartments in Viadana, Bergamo and Milan, as well as the show-room "Alivar" in Milan, a socio-cultural centre in Mazzanati and an industrial complex in Cupromontana.

▶ DANIEL FREIXES

- Barcelona, 1946.
- Studies at the Escuela Superior de Arquitectura in Barcelona, 1970.
- Association with Vicente Miranda, Eulàlia Gonzalez and Pep Anglí, under the name of "Vàris Arquitectes".
- Among his most important works are the Clot Park in Barcelona, the Cinema Museum in Girona and the Corner Bar at the Grand Hyatt Hotel in Potsdamer Platz in Berlin, together with Rafael Moneo.

▶ RON ARAD

- Tel Aviv (Israel), 1951.
- Established in London since 1973, studies at the Architectural Association-School of Architecture until 1979.
- In 1981 together with Dennis Groves and Caroline Thorman he founds his place of work, exhibition and sale of furniture: "One Off".
- Architect, manufacturer of furniture; "Horns Collection" (1986), interior architect; "Bazaar", for Gaultier, designer; "Volumes Collection" (1988)

Kristian Gavoille

Brazaville
- Between 1986 and 1991 collaboration with Philippe Starck.
- From 1988 Disform (Spain) and Neotu (France) start to produce his furniture.
- Among his most recent works are the restaurants of the firms Cartier and Kookaï, Claude Montana's shop in Singapore, as well as sets for France 2, France 3 and the ARTE chain.

Allies and Morrison

- The studio was founded in 1984 by Bob Allies and Graham Morrison after their project was commissioned for the square opposite the National Gallery of Scotland in Edinburgh.
- At present more than 20 people work at the studio, 16 of which are architects.
- Among their works are; the British Embassy in Dublin, a park in Pierhead, a commercial park in Sheffield and work at the Tate Gallery, the Place Theatre and the Horniman Museum.

Mohamed Salahudin Consulting Engineering Bureau

- The MSCEB studio was founded in Bahrain in 1970.
- The studio takes on architectural projects as well as landscaping or civil, mechanical and electrical engineering projects.
- Among the works carried out by MSCEB are Jasmi's Restaurant, Toyota Training Centre, the Jawad Commercial Complex or the BALTECO communications centre, all of which are located in Bahrain.
- The architects responsible for the Taco Maker restaurant are *Gautam Ramesh Mundkur* (India,1957) and *Sadashiv Bhasker Karpe* (India,1945).

Masaharu Takasaki

- Kagoshima, 1953.
- Studies at the University of Meijo, 1976.
- First prize "The Japan Architect" International

House Design Competition in 1977.
- Work as lecturer at Stuttgart and Graz universities
- Founding of the Takasaki Monobito Institute.
- Masaharu Takasaki architects was founded in 1990.
- Among his works are the Kihokucho Astronomical Museum in Kagoshima and the Earth Architecture building in Tokyo.

Dietmar Eberle and Karl Baumschlager

- *Dietmar Eberle*, E. Hittisau, 1952.
- Studies at the Tech. Hochschule in Vienna, 1978.

- *Karl Baumschlager*, Breganz, 1956.
- Studies at the Studium Industrie Design and at the Hochschule f. Angewandte Kunst with H. Hollein, W. Holzbauer and O.M. Ungers, 1982.

- Eberle and Baumschlager set up an office together in 1984.
- Among their works are; the Lagerhalle Holz-Altenreid in Hergartz, the Alcatel building in Lustenau, the Elektro Graf building in Dornbirn and various detached houses in Austria.

Pilar Líbano

- Barcelona.
- Studies of interior architecture at IADE and MASSANA in Barcelona, 1978, 1980.
- Her own studio was set up in 1982.
- Among her works are the bars Star Winds, Back Fire, the discotheques Cibeles and Costa Breve and the shops Antonio Miro, Japan, Groc and Polo Sur, all of which are in Barcelona.